JOHN ROBERT GREGG

JOHN ROBERT

GREGG

*A biography of the shorthand
inventor, educator, publisher and
humanitarian, whose achievements
enriched the lives of millions*

Leslie Cowan PhD FNGA MSc

THE PRE-RAPHAELITE PRESS AT OXFORD 1984

Published by The Pre-Raphaelite Press at Oxford, Ltd.,
51 Wellington Street, Oxford OX2 6BB, England.

ISBN 0 947635 00 9

Printed in Britain by Thomas Leach, Ltd., 54 Ock Street,
Abingdon, Oxon, OX14 5DE, England.

Bound by J. W. Braithwaite & Son Ltd., Commercial Road,
Wolverhampton, WV1 3QX, England.

Contents

Illustrations

Preface

It is an honor to be asked to contribute a few lines of appreciation of this volume written by an outstanding scholar of the shorthand system that bears the name of John Robert Gregg.

Dr Cowan's knowledge of and devotion to Gregg Shorthand will be an inspiration to all students of the System. His exhaustive study of the available material concerning Mr Gregg's professional life is important for all to know. It is with respect and admiration that I congratulate Dr Cowan on his ability to present this material with enthusiasm and accuracy.

It is especially appropriate that this book should come at the present time — so near the one-hundreth anniversary of the publication of the world-renowned System known as Gregg.

JANET K. GREGG-HOWELL

Acknowledgements

I wish to acknowledge, with grateful thanks, the valuable help received from Janet K. Gregg-Howell, and to express my appreciation of her warm approval of my efforts in preparing this biography. I am indebted to the Keeper of Manuscripts, New York Public Library, and to the staff who assisted me during many months of reading; similarly, I wish to thank Miss P. M. Baker, Keeper of the William J. Carlton shorthand collection at the Sterling Library, University of London, England, for much help in locating books, journals and documents throughout the last two years. In my research I received immeasurable assistance from the late Louis A. Leslie, and enjoyed the benefit of unrestricted access to his collection of shorthand publications.

I extend sincere thanks to the many members of the National Shorthand Reporters Association who have shared their memories with me, and to the teachers who responded to my inquiries.

I am grateful to Janet K. Gregg-Howell, and to the late Louis A. Leslie for permission to reproduce photographs.

My special thanks to Tom Colverson who has acted as editor and consultant to the production.

L. C.

Chapter One Childhood, Youth, and a Creation of Genius

When the British Government imposed a reorganisation of administration upon the Scottish highlands in the second half of the 18th century, the McGreggor clan refused to relinquish its territorial authority and was proscribed as 'outlawed'. Forbidden to use the name McGreggor, many of the clan took refuge in the lowlands of Scotland, where they usually adopted the name of Grieg, while others settled in Ireland, and called themselves Gregg. One of the descendants of the latter expatriots was Robert Gregg, who in 1864 accepted a position as station-master at Bushford railway station, Rockcorry, then in Northern Ireland.[1] Several of Robert Gregg's children were noted for their exceptional intelligence, and two of them, Robert junior and Fanny, were regarded as 'brilliant' by their teachers, but it was the youngest child, John Robert Gregg, who achieved international fame as Shorthand Inventor, Educator, and Publisher.

On June 17 1867 John Robert was born at the three-roomed house which the family occupied at Shantonagh, and there he spent the first five years before the family settled at Rockcorry. His parents, Robert and Margaret[2] Gregg, were stern Presbyterians who enforced a domestic discipline which would, by modern standards, be regarded as harsh, yet they were devoted to the welfare of their children. The father was a man of ideas, constrained by the economic and social conditions of his environment. It was he who first conceived the design of the egg-tray with individual wooden compartments, and sold them to the shops and distributors. One of John Robert Gregg's earliest memories was of being allowed to assist in providing the nails for these egg-trays. The father's enterprise prospered until the regrettable occasion when he boasted of his success at the local inn—thereafter, the farmers copied his design and undermined his market.

John joined the little village school in August, 1872. The day was made notable by the address to the assembled children, in which the master anticipated wonderful educational attainments to match those of the brother and sister who had preceded him. That expression of good will is the only one ever recorded of a schoolmaster who was better remembered for his sadistic cruelty. During John's second day at school the master heard him whispering with the boy who shared his form, and instead of issuing a reprimand, he crashed the children's heads together so violently that he severely damaged John's hearing. Fearful of further trouble—the wrath of his father—he did not report this incident, and the injury went untreated. Because he heard only a portion of what was said, and responded irregularly, it was supposed that he was slow-witted at school and at home. Before long in his own family circle he was being talked of as 'poor John', the backward child of whom little could be expected.

In 1877 the Gregg family was visited at the weekend by one of the father's intellectual friends, a journalist called Annesley. On Sunday he accompanied them to the village church where there was first a stir of interest on account of the stranger himself, then excited attention when he took out his notebook to record the sermon in Pitman shorthand. None of the congregation had ever witnessed shorthand writing before. The minister's reaction exceeded that of any one else: he stuttered, hesitated, exhibited the greatest agitation, and barely managed to stumble to the end of the sermon. As soon as the service was over, he rushed to where Mr Annesley stood on the grass in front of the church and begged him not to publish the sermon which he had just reported: it was not his own, he had 'borrowed' it from a leading preacher of the day. This incident, with its promise of the power and usefulness of shorthand, made a deep impression on father Gregg. He determined that his children would benefit from this skill. Accordingly, the two oldest boys, Samuel and Jared, were supplied with Pitman's *Manual of Phonography* which they struggled through without enthusiasm. Subsequently, the two 'brilliant' middle children, Robert junior and Fanny, tried to teach themselves Pitman shorthand, but abandoned the project in disgust.

Isaac Pitman's *Phonography,* published in 1837, was the first system of shorthand to be given wide publicity in England. Particularly during the years near the mid-century, the inventor's brothers propagated the system with evangelical fervour throughout the country, giving free lectures and demonstrations. Very large numbers of people were caught up in the enthusiasm of the moment for the novel interest, and began learning Isaac Pitman's Phonography, but relatively few persisted with the complex system long enough to gain sufficient fluency or speed to make any practical use of the subject.

Until the expansion in commercial communication, which coincided with the introduction of the typewriter in the later 1880s, there was little demand for shorthand clerks in British business life, and the number of shorthand writers engaged in reporting in Parliament and the law courts was exceedingly small. The great majority of persons who undertook the study of shorthand did so with the intention of acquiring a skill for personal use. Although the older-established systems of Gurney and Taylor had gained respect and a body of staunch supporters, they did not attract the public attention like the much-advertised Pitman Phonography. Indeed, a great many people who studied Pitman Phonography naively believed that Isaac Pitman had invented shorthand writing and the word 'Phonography'.

In Isaac Pitman's system the phonetic elements of speech are represented by signs derived from the segments of the circle. Some of these signs are written lightly and others heavily (or 'shaded') to differentiate meanings. The signs for consonants are linked together to form the skeletons of words from which the vowels have been omitted, and those vowels are indicated principally by dots marked beside the consonantal skeleton after it has been written. In the interest of economy of form, the simple phonetic combinations of signs are modified by a large number of rules, and exceptions to those rules, comparable with the inflections of a language. The complexity increases as the student progresses, and for most of the learners these proved too discouraging to allow them to master the theory and proceed to speed-building. It was so with the older Gregg children.

John was exempt from the mandatory shorthand learning: for John was 'simple'. In later life he was to comment how deeply he felt the stigma of the universal opinion that he was incapable of worthwhile achievement and doomed to the bleakest of future prospects. But even at the age of ten he was already possessed of the powers of determination and persistence which marked his adult life. He decided that he would learn shorthand and prove to himself, and others, that he could gain a skill which was denied to those reputed to be cleverer than himself. He would teach himself shorthand—but not Pitman shorthand, which caused such pains to his brothers and sisters.

John investigated the textbooks and chose the slimmest volume obtainable, *Odell's Shorthand,* which consisted of twenty pages of text and two charts. It was priced at 8d (13c), but because it was second-hand, he got it half-price, thus saving four valuable pennies. He began the study and found it fascinating, and realised that he could easily cope with the system. It was for the boy a great personal achievement. In his own words: 'I could teach myself shorthand because it didn't involve hearing.'

The system sold under the name of Odell (the publisher) was in fact the famous system of Samuel Taylor,[3] first published in 1786. It was highly regarded by professional shorthand writers on account of its fluency and the absence or shading and position-writing (the compulsory location of outlines above, on, or below the line of writing to indicate different meanings for the same outline).

Curiously, John's success went unacknowledged by his family. By now shorthand was a distasteful subject to the older children, and if his parents took any notice of his writing, they probably scorned it as the wild scribbling of a backward child. The parents' worst fears regarding his intelligence were confirmed by his school reports which term after term, and year after year, recorded John Robert Gregg at the bottom of his class. During the six years which he spent at Rockcorry school he learned little, for he heard little. Moreover, his schoolmaster had developed a particular animosity towards the boy who failed to fulfil his educational prophecy.

Shorthand had brought to John the joy of knowledge— it had also given him an interest and the means to better himself. He delved into books about shorthand systems and the lives of shorthand writers and authors, and discovered shorthand journals. He had begun to educate himself through shorthand.

There were, however, other boyhood fascinations. He witnessed a performance of tightrope walking by the famous Frenchman, Blondin, and was immensely impressed. It was shortly after Blondin had amazed the world by daring to cross the Niagara Falls by a rope strung 160 feet above the water. Young John then set about developing his powers of balance by practising upon a rope secured to posts in his back yard. He would often exercise his skill by walking several miles along the railway line without once touching the earth below. Like most of his occupations, that was kept from his parents, who would have been aghast, for two years before John was born, one of their infant children had been killed by a passing train.

In 1878 the Gregg family moved to Glasgow, the principal commercial and industrial city of Scotland. It is not known what occupation the father followed, but his address at North Street, beside a busy railway complex, suggests that he continued to work for a railway company. By now Samuel, the oldest son, had married and moved to Liverpool, in England, where he worked in an architect's or builder's office. Fanny and George, the children next in age to John, were delicate—already marked out for that disease which nineteenth-century families dreaded, tuberculosis.

They were certainly poor, and all the children had to contribute to the family income. John, too, had to be found some paid employment, so it happened that the person who was to influence the education of tens of millions of young people ended his school days before his thirteenth birthday.

A very important incident occurred in John's life at this time. An elderly family friend, whose opinions were deeply respected, called on the Greggs and put some question to the boy. When he failed to hear, one of the other children reminded the visitor that 'John is hard of hearing'. The old man patted him on the head and remarked with emphasis: 'Ah! Laddie—hard o' hearing, but no' hard in the head'. It was the first time that any one of importance had expressed confidence in John's intelligence. He was overjoyed. Many years later he averred that those six words changed the course of his childhood: they gave him solid grounds for trusting to his own latent ability.

His parents placed him in the office of lawyer called Ritchie, not as an articled clerk to learn the profession through an apprenticeship, but as an office boy, whose wages for working six days a week from 9 a.m. to 6 p.m. were five shillings. (One dollar per week, at the then current rate of exchange).

Mr Ritchie was highly regarded in his profession, but he was frequently diverted from his practice by his love of conviviality and his unquenchable thirst, so his business operations were erratic, with long intervals between cases. He had family or business connections with America and acted as an advisor in matters of trans-Atlantic litigation and commercial investment. His principal requirements were for someone to receive and sort the mail; to receive callers; and to examine the *Glasgow Herald* for announcements of opportunities for financial investment. His employee was happy to accommodate him in these light duties, and thankful to find that the greater part of his day was left free for the pursuit of his personal interests.

Glasgow offered enormous educational advantages over the little Irish village. John grasped the opportunities by reading in the free libraries and attending the free lectures. It was one such course of introductory demonstration lectures on Pitman Phonography, at the old Athenaeum in 1879, which stimulated him to study that shorthand system. Of course he had no money to pay for the classes which were intended to follow the lectures, so he had to be his own teacher. He accomplished that by studying Pitman textbooks at the splendidly stocked Mitchell Library, close to his parents' house. He did not like Isaac Pitman's Phonography: he was critical of the need to strip words of their vowels and to apply an intricate theory prior to forming the geometric outlines, and he compared these with the simple though clumsy outlines of Taylor's system.

The British Pitman writers were sufficiently numerous to support a variety of shorthand journals, and it was probably by reading articles in these that John's attention was drawn to the Continental European systems, almost all of which rejected the severely geometrical alphabet of the Pitman system. In those days Pitman adherents were ferocious in their denunciation of every other system, and their intolerance was usually regarded as a virtue by those who knew only one system. However, John was already in a position to consider the merits and failings of two shorthand systems, and he proceeded to inquire into the Continental preferences and to form his own opinions. In 1883 he saved his pennies until he had amassed sufficient to buy a copy of the textbook of the English adaption of a system invented by the Frenchman Emile Duployé (1868) and published in Britain by John Matthew Sloan,[4] as *Sloan's Duployan Shorthand,* (1883).

Duployé had based his alphabet on the cursive, or flowing, lines of longhand writing, and had included the vowels within the outlines. He had designed his system to be easily learned and applied to personal use in place of longhand, and had brought it to public attention through a massive advertising campaign. It met with considerable success in France. J. M. Sloan attempted to repeat the popularisation programme in Britain by employing newspaper announcements and posters promising the student a writing speed of 100 words per minute within two months, in return for two hours' study per day. Unfortunately, Sloan's adaption to the English language was not wholly satisfactory, as the British writers were to discover. Nevertheless, John found the system preferable to those he already knew, and for some years used it for all his lecture notes, extracts from books, and personal records.

In the course of his reading John learned that there were two other English adaptions of Duployé shorthand: one by the American Mrs H. A. Pernin of Detroit, Michigan, and the other by Jean P. A. Martin of Lyons, France. Each of the adaptations introduced modifications which were felt most appropriate to the English language. John thoroughly studied these adaptations, so that at the age of sixteen he had mastered three different systems of shorthand, and was familiar with two variations of the system he regularly used.

At his employer's office John found little interest in the law papers which passed through his hands, except on the rare occasions when Mr Ritchie was involved with some case of dramatic nature. But he did acquire a familiarity with legal terminology which was to be useful to him later in life. The office was at West Regent Street, right at the heart of that territory occupied by the leading commercial and legal firms, and thronged with young office workers and junior executives. Soon the tall youth, with the mass of ginger hair topped by a Scottish bonnet with its twin ribbons, was well-known. He made friends with the American consul and his staff, who occupied an office in the same block, and he mixed socially with a group of young Australian men who were pioneering the shipping of frozen lamb to Britain.

15

Several circumstances predisposed John to American interests: his visits to the consular office gave him access to American magazines and newspapers which were the more attractive to him because he knew something of American life and literature from his shorthand magazines; moreover, at the lawyer's office he had found a large quantity of American books, and a long run of *Scribner's Magazine* dealing with the events of the Civil War. Initially John was drawn to the latter because his brother George was deeply interested in the life of General Grant; afterwards he discovered the fascination of History and made good use of his plentiful leisure at the office to read deeply on American affairs. Possessed of an excellent memory, he made himself an expert in the history of the American Civil War in the course of several years study.

Throughout 1882 and 1883 John advanced his education by a great deal of reading during the day, and afterwards at the Mitchell Library, and at the free lectures given at the University of Glasgow. His conscientious and methodical manner of accumulating information is attested by the lecture notes on logic delivered by Professor Veitch and Mr Andrew, and recorded in well-written Sloan-Duployan shorthand, dated 1883.

Shorthand preoccupied John's thoughts. He followed the debates and disputes which raged in the popular magazine *Exchange and Mart* concerning the merits of rival shorthand theories, and he read with care the expansion published in book form afterwards edited by the authority on the science and history of shorthand, the Glasgow court reporter, Thomas Anderson. By his own account John read and reread Anderson's *History of Shorthand* (1882) which critically surveyed many systems from antiquity to modern times, and he pondered long over the five principles which the author laid down as appropriate to the 'Shorthand of the Future'.

The same writer had commented on the great progress which had been made by the two leading German shorthand systems—so John had to investigate them. He did this by studying Richter's English adaption of the Gabelsberger, and Michaelis' adaption of the Stolze systems. Both rejected the geometric for the curved characters which follow the longhand slant, but used meandering movements which were the common German manner of writing at that time.

His passion for shorthand was such that when he went for a summer vacation to stay with his brother at Liverpool, he spent a good part of his time at the reading room of the Picton Library, gathering information which was not available in Glasgow. He maintained a correspondence, in shorthand, with eminent foreign writers and court reporters, including Mrs Pernin and Mr Martin. Once, Mrs Pernin offered him the British agency for her textbooks. It was his first business offer, but one which had to be refused. None of those taking part in the scholarly exchanges knew that their correspondent was a boy of seventeen.

In 1884 John attended a lecture in Glasgow given by Isaac Pitman. He was astonished at the reverence paid to the aged inventor and his system, for he, himself, was very critical of the Pitman system and could not share in their feelings. By then he was seriously dissatisfied with every system he knew.

In order to further his knowledge of the American scene, he wrote to a number of publishers to obtain sample journals. Among those that he received was the July issue of Browne and Holland's *Shorthand News* which contained a biographical account which was to inspire and direct his youthful ambitions. The article told of the heroic efforts of Dr Thierry Mieg, a Moroccan physician, to invent the ideal rational shorthand system of the future. The 63-year-old enthusiast had devoted the whole of his lifetime's leisure to this one pursuit—so far without success. John was particularly struck by one sentence: 'He has adopted the slope of the ordinary writing which will survive as the most beautiful of all'. Fiftyfour years later at the conference in London honouring the Golden Jubilee of the publication of the first Gregg shorthand textbook, he reminisced:

> That brief statement made a profound impression on me. Coming upon it soon after reading Thomas Anderson's books in which the same opinion was expressed, it isn't perhaps, too much to say that it was the deciding factor in determining the lines on which all my future experiments should be made. I decided to make a fresh start by experimenting along the lines of a system on the slope of longhand, without shading, without position-writing, and with connecting vowels.

The system he had resolved to construct would be superior in ease of learning and facility of writing to all others. It was intended entirely for his own use. Now the long intervals between his lawyer's office visits were occupied almost wholly with the analysis of shorthand alphabets and the testing of new characters and outlines, and after 6 o'clock he continued at the Mitchell Library, surrounded by pamphlets and journals of the systems he knew.

In view of John Robert Gregg's activities it is amazing that his parents continued to believe that he was 'simple'; but they did. In part, they did not know of his serious studies, and in part they were too deeply entrenched in their first opinion. His parents seem to have interpreted his shorthand ability as the accomplishment of an Idiot Savant. In his absence, they continued to speak of 'poor John'. His mother wrote into her will that the oldest son should retain John's share of her savings, and that it should be offered to him only in small quantities.

The Gregg parents had many troubles to distract their attention from their youngest child: the next in age, George, was seriously ill with tuberculosis by the age of 22, and in a final attempt to improve his health they shipped him to New Zealand. They were worried, too, about the delicate health of their only daughter, Fanny. She, doubtless in sympathy with John's disability, had joined the Institute for the Deaf and Dumb at Glasgow, and qualified there as a teacher. John was closest to her, and she alone realised his potential. He consulted her particularly in problems concerning the phonetic analysis of speech, and it was she who provided him with the simplified vowel classification which he used for Gregg Shorthand.

John early displayed the characteristics of a born teacher who, having taken joy in the acquisition of knowledge, wishes to pass it on to others. In the Autumn of 1884 he persuaded one of the young Australian businessmen,

Michael Murdoch Andrew, to study shorthand. From a day diary which he kept at this time, it is possible to learn how a small service to a friend was to draw him into the world of education. He went on the 22nd September to purchase the *Duployan Instructor* for Andrew and was sold the fifth edition. He found that it contained disturbing changes in the presentation and rules, and sought out the Sloan-Duployan agent whose address was given at a location near John's legal office. There he talked with Thomas Stratford Malone, who had recently settled in Glasgow, and had organised a shorthand association to propagate the system which he taught. Malone attempted to interest John in shorthand classes and the social activities of the shorthand association—without success, for John could afford neither—but he was brought into contact with other shorthand writers for the first time. Meanwhile, he coached Mr Andrew and subsequently his business colleague, Finley Hogarth, before both left for London.

John extended his shorthand interests by an acquaintance with two practising shorthand reporters at Glasgow who wrote the Gurney system. They provided him with a fascinating insight into the practical application of shorthand to verbatim writing. Momentarily John must have had some real hope of overcoming his deafness, for it is recorded[5] that he expressed an interest in the prospect of becoming a 'shorthand amanuensis'.[6] But the prerequisite, perfect hearing, was never to be his.

It was some difficulty in obtaining a Sloan-Duployan magazine which caused John to renew acquaintance with Mr Malone at his Shorthand Institute at Hope Street—a grandly titled apartment which served as classroom, meeting hall, and bedroom for its batchelor resident. Thomas Stratford Malone had originally come from Dublin, Southern Ireland, where he had spent some years in a seminary before abandoning his studies because he had ceased to believe in God. When he met J. M. Sloan, he learned something of his system—though he never achieved any fluency or speed—and moved to Glasgow as Sloan's agent for the sale of textbooks. Malone now spoke again of his Association, for he was exceedingly anxious to increase the number of his members. John must have explained that he was unable to pay[7] the entrance and monthly membership fees, for Malone waived these. Undoubtedly he saw in the youth a valuable asset to his Association and his school.

Not long after John began attending the Wednesday evening meetings he learned of the shorthand competition to be held on the 17th June, his eighteenth birthday. When he hesitated to enter, for he had no experience of such activities, Malone condescendingly invited him to sit with his pupils, so that he could 'make a good show for the examiner'. It was John who won the first prize—to the considerable displeasure of Malone who witnessed his carefully tutored students vanquished by an outsider who had never had a shorthand lesson in his life. The *Sloan-Duployan Journal*[8] recorded:

Prize Competition: First prize, John Robert Gregg, whose paper presented carefully traced shorthand notes, at the rate of 85 words per minute, accompanied by a most accurate transcription in longhand.

John received an engraved gold medal[9] which he was to treasure for the greater part of his life. It was presented to him by J. M. Sloan when he visited Glasgow in July, and at that time John wrote for him at the rate of 120 words per minute, and received from him a handwritten note:

I hereby certify that Mr John Robert Gregg, 56 North Street, Glasgow, has a thorough knowledge of Sloan-Duployan Phonography. (signed) 'John Matthew Sloan'.

This was John's authority to start his career as a teacher of shorthand.

Today almost all people, other than shorthand writers, associate shorthand with the preparation for secretarial positions in commerce, and very few know anything of the extensive personal use of shorthand in the past by intellectuals. It is difficult to appreciate how highly prized it was as an accomplishment which saved so much time and energy to countless lawyers, preachers, politicians and authors. In late-nineteenth-century Britain there were shorthand societies in most of the major towns. Numerically they could not be compared with those of France, far less with those of Germany, where almost every professional person had some practical knowledge of the art and was often an active member of a shorthand society.[10] Nevertheless, the British shorthand societies were humming with life and there was endless discussion concerning the merits of rival systems, and in the debates there was a degree of emotional involvement more usually associated with religious disputes.

It is possible to distinguish a number of different types of people who belonged to shorthand associations; most of them had a core of older members who had taken part in the mid-century enthusiasm for Phonography, and subsequently retained an interest in shorthand theory; and there were usually some others drawn to the science of shorthand as an intellectual study. A small proportion were teachers of shorthand, or practising shorthand reporters working for the law courts, but the bulk of the members consisted of those who were in commercial or legal employment, who hoped to enhance their prestige and self-respect through society membership.

At the Wednesday evening meetings of the Sloan-Duployan Association John quickly became an acknowledged authority and won the respect of the other members; it also brought the attentions of Mr Malone, who was ever ready to employ the talents of others to advance his own interests. Malone persuaded him to undertake teaching for him on Tuesday and Friday evenings from 6 to 10 p.m., for which he was paid 5s.3d per week ($1.05); a small amount, but a welcome addition to his meagre budget.

Teaching Sloan-Duployan sharpened John's critical awareness of the system's defects. Within a few weeks he spoke of his dissatisfaction to Malone, comparing the theory with the five principles which Thomas Anderson had laid down as the basic requirements for an ideal system. In summary, Anderson had written:

1. There must be independent characters for the vowels, and they must be adapted for writing in union with the characters representing the consonants.

2. The characters must be written on one slope.
3. There must be no shading.
4. There must be no position-writing.
5. The rules of abbreviation must be sure, comprehensive and few.

This was quite new to Malone. John told him of his own research and how he had been inspired by the *Shorthand News* article on Thierry Mieg. Malone temporarily threw off his habitual melancholy and grew very interested, particularly when John told him that he had made substantial progress towards the invention of a system that would be superior to the Sloan-Duployan.

Malone then spoke of the serious disputes he was having with Sloan, and said that he wanted to resign his agency and would do so if only he had an alternative shorthand to offer his students. John soon after took to Malone samples of his experimental alphabets and the article on Thierry Mieg. The older man asked, and was given permission, to borrow the material so that he could copy a quantity into his commonplace book.

Seeing that he had much to gain from cultivating the friendship of this wonderfully gifted youth, Malone now made flattering comments on John's research and invited him to collaborate with him in the production and publication of a new shorthand system. He spoke of his experience of marketing shorthand, and pointed out that John was penniless and could not hope to see his ideas printed without assistance. He promised that in the proposed shorthand John would be acknowledged as part-author, and that he would share in the rewards. John was delighted with the prospect, and he did not doubt that Malone would honour his promises.

To set the partnership in motion it was agreed that each would draw up an alphabet which could be discussed and criticised. Alas! when John received Malone's alphabet he was dismayed: It was a crude production, devoid of originality. He had given the older man credit for much more knowledge than he possessed. The fact was that Malone knew no other shorthand than Sloan-Duployan, and was totally ignorant of shorthand history and the researches of contemporary inventors, and he knew nothing about such important matters as the frequency of particular phonetic elements in the English language. John realised that it would be he who would have to do the lion's share of the projected work. Nevertheless, the meetings for discussion and criticism took place day by day, and a large quantity of trial alphabets were exchanged after Wednesday association meetings and after evening teaching, and a great deal of writing was done on the blackboard as ideas were hammered out. But Malone was an anxious individual who needed support and reassurance: his lack of self-confidence was now demonstrated when he enrolled the assistance of two shorthand teacher acquaintances[11] to comment on his trial alphabets, and advertised his own weakness when he offered to pay the members of his own association a premium of £2 for good ideas which he could incorporate into his project.

The partners in this venture were ill-matched: John was full of vitality, fluent in the theories of ten systems, urgent and forceful; Malone was slow, dependent on the rules of one system and suspicious of novelty, and fearful of what he had undertaken. While Malone agreed that the new system should be based on the slope of longhand, he could not accept John's suggestion that they abandon 'shading' which was used in Sloan-Duployan; and, worse still, he insisted that they use 'shading' in extremely difficult positions, such as small hooks and circles and upstrokes. He obstinately refused to be guided by John's knowledge of symbols, and insisted that the most frequently used vowel, 'E', be represented by a hook which necessitated outlines with numerous awkward angles. John was disappointed: the many compromises which he had been obliged to make undermined the hopes he had held of a system with an easy regular flow along the line.

The alphabet and the rules were settled and a textbook of instruction was prepared. John read and corrected the manuscript and gave the system the name of *Script*.[12] Malone, in his impatience, had hurried the work, and the production of this new shorthand had occupied little more than a single month. Malone resigned his Sloan-Duployan agency on the 2nd September 1885, and the alphabet of *Script* was copyrighted and registered at Stationers' Hall.[13] Thomas Stratford Malone was described as 'proprietor'; there was no mention of John Robert Gregg as co-author. Malone now offered Script to those who came to his institute in answer to his advertisements for tuition in shorthand, but he had so little confidence in the new system that he wrote a pamphlet[14] in praise of Sloan-Duployan.

When Malone began to attempt to win over the members of his Association to the new shorthand, John found his services were in demand, for it was he who was called upon to explain the novel features of Script and to compare them with Pitman Phonography and other rival systems. While Malone did from time to time reiterate his promise of a share in the rewards, John noticed that he rarely mentioned the joint authorship in the presence of others. True to his character Malone now found a way to avoid personal responsibility for financing the publication and advertising of the new system. He persuaded a body of acquaintances to join with him in floating the 'Script Phonography Company', with himself as Chairman and John as (unpaid) Secretary. This was the first of four companies which Malone floated to propagate Script, and it, like all that followed, brought financial benefit to no one but Malone.

Early in 1886 a Mr Alexander Webster, who had been taught Sloan-Duployan shorthand by Malone in Dublin, settled in Glasgow and was soon involved in the teaching of Script and the activities of the Association. In him Malone found an ally when he decided to amend the newly written Script by the addition of complicating rules. John's strenuous opposition to these was met with Malone's aloof coldness, and an ostentatious transfer of favour to Webster.

John's share in the preparation of Script had brought him only one reward: the clearer understanding of what was required in a sound shorthand system, and he now returned to his own experiments with greater determination than ever to create that 'ideal system'. He would follow the five fundamental principles laid down by Anderson, but in addition he would employ the most desirable elements which he had found in the French, German and American shorthand systems. His system would be phonetic, would have vowels joined in their natural order, and would be based on the longhand slope employed by Gabelsberger and Stolze, while using the horizontal flow of Taylor. He would avoid the position-writing, the shading, and the complex rules of Pitman, and similarly there would be none of Duployé's confusing multiple characters, nor Script's angular crudities. In his intensive research John reviewed the strengths and weaknesses of hundreds of alphabets, and by a process of elimination concentrated upon those which were primarily curvilinear. In this choice he was undoubtedly influenced by his admiration for the appearance of the handwriting displayed in an American magazine which he regularly studied, the *Western Penman.*

Curiously, it was through one of Malone's efforts to win favour for Script that John was provided with an essential catalyst for the formation of his own theory. Malone had gone to discuss Script with William Pettigrew, a respected shorthand authority in Glasgow, and a leader in the community, but Malone had failed to make any progress because he could not deal with the technicalities of theory brought in argument against him. He brought in John as an expert adviser to cross swords with the able exponent of the systems at his confectionery store on busy Sauchiehall Street.

Alderman[15] Pettigrew delighted to talk about shorthand theory: in his youth he had been one of the pioneers of Isaac Pitman's Phonography when it was first enthusiastically received among educated people, but subsequently he had discovered serious weaknesses in that system and had attempted to correct them in a system of his own published in 1864. His own system had not been well received by the public, but he remained deeply interested in shorthand. Pettigrew listened to John's exposition and he conceded that Script appeared to offer some advantages over Pitman's shorthand, but he harshly criticised those awkward joinings of horizontal and upward characters which were common to Script and Pitman—joinings which could not be kept distinct and legible except by an extreme reduction in the speed of writing.

When John returned to his alphabetic experiments he was reminded of Alderman Pettigrew's denunciation of obtuse angles, and the thought occurred to him that he could turn these problem joinings to his own advantage: as the two straight lines tended to become obscured in combination and to take on the appearance of curves, why not represent these frequent combinations of sounds by large curves. Such curves are easily written and are not subject to distortion at speed, yet they are instantly recognisable. It was simple, but no one in the history of shorthand had ever applied this principle before. John now worked with feverish energy by night and day compiling tables of letter and sound combinations and testing them with blends.

His continuing thoughts about character blends now led him to a brilliant idea which was to distinguish his alphabet from all that had previously been formed: his entire alphabet of shorthand characters would be constructed to give *facility in combination* of characters, one with the other. In the past the most scientific of the shorthand inventors had allocated to the most common sounds the most easily written shorthand characters, but they had never thought of building up a shorthand alphabet on the basis of giving the easiest *combinations of characters* to the most frequently recurring speech sounds. John now applied himself to a most exhaustive investigation of character combinations which were natural to the human hand. He also became convinced that many of the most facile movements were based on the portions of the ellipse and he deliberately applied its graceful curves to the greater number of his characters. Finally, he settled upon his alphabet:

A segment of the ellipse, tilted on the diagonal, provided the shorthand character for the consonant 'P'.

Because the number of easily written single-stroke characters is so limited, all shorthand inventors had to allocate more than one sound to some of the characters. Pitman shorthand, in common with many other systems, distinguished between 'paired' characters by 'shading'. John, having rejected 'shading', used a difference of size. Thus the curve which represents 'P' was written larger, to represent 'B'.

The right segment of the ellipse provided the characters for 'F', and for 'V' when that curve was written larger.

A section of the ellipse written horizontally as a convex curve provided the character for 'K' as in 'Cat' and, when written larger, the same curve was used to represent the hard 'G' as in 'Good'.

When written with the concave curve, the character is used to represent the 'R' sound, and written larger, to represent 'L'.

These characters can be combined to produce elegant and useful blends.

Experiments had determined that horizontal and obliquely struck forward strokes were among the most facile to hand. John used them to represent 'N' and 'M', and 'T' and 'D' (written upwards).

These characters can be combined to form other useful blends.

For the frequently used 'S' sound, as in 'Sat', John used the familiar shape of the comma applied in ordinary punctuation. Because the 'S' is so frequently joined to other letters of the alphabet, he gave to this shorthand character a special flexibility by allowing it to be written both in a clockwise and an anti-clockwise motion.

Straight downward-written strokes, differentiated by three sizes, were allocated to the sounds of 'SH', as in 'short'; 'CH', as in 'church'; and 'J', as in 'judge'.

In earlier shorthand systems the vowels were considered less important than the consonants, and were frequently omitted or indicated by disjoined marks written after the skeleton outline formed from the connected consonants. But in John's shorthand the vowels were regarded as specially important—they were to be immediately recognisable. While he was pondering on the most suitable shape to give these vowels and how he might classify them he talked of their treatment in the Sloan-Duployan textbook with Mr Annesley, his father's friend, who, years before, had first demonstrated shorthand to him. Now Mr Annesley challenged the accuracy of that system's treatment of vowels so vigorously that they consulted with John's sister, Fanny, to have the benefit of her experience in teaching vowels to deaf children. Afterwards the discussion was continued with Fanny, and she suggested how he might approach the problem of obtaining a simple but soundly phonetic arrangement of vowels in his own system.

The vowels were separated into four groups, and the most easily written characters are assigned to the most frequently recurring sounds. For the lingual vowels (ă, ä, ā, ĭ, ĕ, ē), mainly formed by the tongue, circles are used; for labial vowels (ŏ, aw, ō, ŭ, ŏŏ, ōō), mainly formed by the lips, hooks are used.[16]

The small circle is used to represent

ĭ as in 'pit'	o
and ĕ as in 'pet'	ǫ
and ē as in 'peat'	ǫ̸

The larger circle is used to represent

ă as in 'at'	O
and ä as in 'art'	Ǫ
and ā as in 'ate'	Ǫ̸

The small upward hook is used to represent

ŏ as in 'hot'	U
and ö as in 'orb'	Ụ
and ō as in 'oar'	Ụ̸

The small downward hook is used to represent

ŭ as in 'tuck'	∩
and ŏŏ as in 'took'	∩̣
and ōō as in 'tomb'	∩̸

Almost all John's work on the shorthand system was done at his legal office where he was left undisturbed by his employer's continued thirst for Scotch whisky and his preference for the company of his drinking companions. The family home was now blighted by illness: in March 1886 they learned that George Gregg had died of tuberculosis in New Zealand, a few days before his 24th birthday; then, before they could adjust to that loss, they found that the only daughter, Fanny, was incurably ill of the same disease. Her condition rapidly deteriorated, and by the Spring of 1887—when John finalised his alphabet—she was desperately sick. To the very great grief of the family, Fanny died in June 1887, at the age of 27.

John was so upset that he could not concentrate on shorthand experiments. He wrapped up the research notes of the previous ten months, and attempted to alleviate his depression by a little journalism. He took part in a hotly debated controversy in the correspondence section of the *Glasgow Citizen* concerning the supposed limitations of shorthand speed, and he competed for, and won, a journalistic prize offered for the best excerpt from an American publication. Immediately afterwards he was commissioned to provide a newspaper column that offered advice to the love-lorn.

Such activities, however, were temporary diversions. He now had to think seriously about his future. He took stock of the uncertain prospects of Malone's Institute where the pupils were few, and the promised share of the rewards from Script shorthand which had not materialised. He knew that Malone was eager to introduce Script to the heavily populated English provinces, and he now felt he could combine a desire to leave Glasgow with an ambitious adventure which could improve his own position: he suggested to Malone that he could move to Liverpool, where his eldest brother lived, on the understanding that he should be 'sole agent' for Script shorthand in that area. Malone was only too pleased to accept this suggestion. An agreement was drawn up and signed on the 1st August, 1887, whereby John was to receive one half of the profits of the sale of Script shorthand textbooks, and was free to set up a school of his own in England.

Malone was delighted to be relieved of the embarrassment of John's presence in Glasgow, but other shorthand enthusiasts were sorry to lose him. The Glasgow Shorthand Writers Association presented him with an illuminated address which reads:

We, the members of the Glasgow Shorthand Writers Association having learned of your approaching departure from Glasgow, desire to convey to you our most cordial wishes for your future welfare, and hereby to record our appreciation of the services which, in your secretarial capacity and otherwise, you have rendered to our cause, and interests, with uniform cheerfulness, courtesy, and patience. We are pleased to know that in another great centre, affording you still larger scope for your talents and energies, you are about to raise the flag of progress on behalf of a noble art, and thus, that although removed from us by distance, the link of a common cause and sympathy will still remain.

CHAPTER NOTES

1. Rockcorry was subsequently incorporated into the Irish Republic.

2. Née Courney Johnson.

3. By coincidence Isaac Pitman had also studied Taylor's system in the edition by Harding.

4. John Matthew Sloan, 1858-1929.

5. A statement by Mr Malone in April, 1888.

6. A shorthand amanuensis was a reporter's assistant.

7. John's pay at this time was 9 shillings per week (less than $2).

8. July 15, 1885. The passage dictated was a political speech.

9. He was to wear this medal upon a watch-chain for 50 years or more, until the link wore away, and the medal dropped off and was never recovered.

10. In 1889 there were 703 shorthand societies in Germany devoted to the Gabelsberger system—the most popular of the several competing systems.

11. Mr Robie, of Strathbungo, and Mr Cranston, of Edinburgh.

12. The word 'script' was a European term for writing which ran along a single slope.

13. November 4, 1885.

14. *Revolution in Shorthand,* published September 22, 1885.

15. 'Alderman' was the honorary title given to the senior elected member of the local government.

16. As an aid to learning, two small marks (diacriticals) were used under the vowels. John believed that in practical writing it was not necessary to distinguish the three sounds in each vowel group. Because his vowels and consonants are joined, there is seldom any doubt in reading the vowels. The experience of countless millions of Gregg Shorthand writers proved him correct in his early conviction.

Chapter Two Trials and Troubles

Having settled-in with his oldest brother at the suburb of Formby, John's first priority was to get an inexpensive office in central Liverpool. He found a small room on the top floor of a commercial property at 62 Dale Street, and described it in his first advertising leaflet as 'The Script Phonography Institute'. With energy and youthful zest John set about whipping up interest in the shorthand system. He handed out thousands of handbills, inserted many small advertisements in the local newspapers, called upon large numbers of school teachers and educational officials and journalists. Whenever and wherever he got the opportunity he talked with all who would listen to him of the advantages of writing shorthand. Although he did not then realise it, John was a remarkable salesman. His enthusiasm and undoubted sincerity of commitment to the art of shorthand impressed those who spoke with him, and his command of his subject counterbalanced his lack of experience.

Soon he was selling copies of the Script textbook and enrolling pupils for evening tuition and persuading them to subscribe to the *Script Phonography Journal* edited by Malone. His teaching was individual, intensive and skilful, and the first pupils made such good progress that they were happy to leave testimonials or recommend others from among their relatives or friends. The speed at which the Script students acquired a working knowledge of shorthand astonished those who knew the older systems, and this was achieved despite the inherent weaknesses foisted upon the system by Malone's insistence on ill-advised Sloan-Duployan principles. To a large extent John's successful results followed from his excellence as a teacher, but in part it was because he modified the system as presented in the textbook by omitting the clumsy position-writing which undermined the students' speed and fluency.

John wrote frequently to Malone and the members of the Modern Shorthand Association at Glasgow, giving news of his developing school and his circle of teachers and journalists who, after tuition, remained his close acquaintances and were pleased to broadcast the benefits to be derived from shorthand. In return Malone sent a succession of dismal letters in which he blamed his lack of progress upon the prejudice of the city and the lethargy of his associates, and the adverse propaganda of rival systems.

Malone had not expected John to make a success of the Liverpool venture so he was truly amazed to learn that the youth had won the confidence of established Pitman teachers and had arranged the adoption of Script at leading educational institutes within weeks. On the 20th November, 1887, he wrote: 'The opening of Birkenhead school is brilliant work for so short a time. The fellows here are lauding Gregg for pluck'. On the 8th December, he wrote:

Your having nailed the Manchester and Liverpool teachers is good news indeed. I have tried every art in Glasgow to get some of them the length of looking into it, but in

27

vain. In fact, we can not get them to read a single line of pamphlet or circular while at the same time they join in a chorus of denunciation of the system louder and more savage now than ever.

Malone, whose dull plodding teaching produced only mediocre results, was particularly struck by the rapidity with which John's students achieved high standards of ability. On the 18th January, 1888, he wrote to John: 'Your note of the 17th instant with its astonishing and most welcome intelligence to hand. The results reflect the utmost credit on your office and are additional pillars to the system. If you send us copies we will put them up here and otherwise make telling use of them'.

Within a few weeks of the new year John had disquieting news of Malone's activities in Glasgow in connection with the Script Phonography Company. The small capital supplied by Malone's acquaintances was spent and Malone was trying to attract the support of financiers for a new limited liability company. John inquired what was afoot, but Malone demurred, then revealed that it was his intention 'to sell the copyright of the system to a company with £4,000 capital—myself to be paid a bulk sum and appointed General Manager'. John's acquaintances at the Modern Shorthand Association, now having reason to distrust Malone's integrity, warned that Malone was planning to manoeuvre him out of his financial interest in the system.

As the agreement was coming up for renewal in August, John wrote to Malone concerning the extension of his agency, wishing to learn how Malone proposed to safeguard his co-authorship interests. But Malone, urgently trying to hurry on a transfer of responsibility to the 'new company', would not be drawn: 'Regarding the extension of agencies: tis out of my power now to consider it as the reconstruction scheme is now before the capitalists with whom I have no communication, and you can at once see that I can make no changes pending these negotiations'.[1]

On 27th February, John wrote to Malone:

Owing to the unforeseen event of the purchase of the copyright of Script Phonography, I am anxious to learn that you have in some definite way secured my interests in the system. If you retain the copyright, I am, of course, willing to rely on your promises of future rewards according to the success of the system, but I can not be expected to do so with a company.

But Malone was determined to repudiate John's connection with the invention of Script: on the 11th March 1888, Malone wrote that he protested against 'Any shape of permanent claims being suspended over my head like the sword of Damocles; a vague, mysterious debt to be brought up again and again'. Malone was prepared to offer John an extension of territory and implied that the agency was his promised reward.

John was outraged by the treachery of the man. He had worked enormously hard for the Script cause: in the first six months he had sold 1800 textbooks and enrolled 100 students, and he had learned that Malone had used such results to persuade business men that there was enormous potential for the system and had organised a new company which was about to undermine his financial position. He wrote to Malone:[2]

Probably no one but yourself would accuse me of being such a fool as to regard the appointment of extended territory as remuneration for the services I have rendered. . On reviewing our whole connection I now see clearly that it was your deliberate intention from the first, not to fulfil your promises. . . . Since coming here I have devoted, I may say, almost every waking moment to the propagation of the system, and have devoted every penny of surplus to advertising it—yet on the eve of success I leave all rather than serve under the banner of one who has treated me so dishonestly. . . . . In conclusion, I regret that your letters and conduct leave me (in justice to myself) no alternative but resignation, and in particular I regret the severance from my former colleagues for many of whom I have the greatest esteem.

Malone had not expected this resignation which could have an extremely prejudicial influence upon his efforts to transfer his copyright to a company in exchange for £1,500, the salaried position as managing director, and a royalty on the sale of textbooks. He immediately dispatched his assistant, Alexander Webster, to Liverpool to talk with John. Webster was instructed to persuade, and if that failed to bribe, and if that failed to threaten. John, however, resisted all his efforts and plainly told him that he would withdraw his resignation only if Malone conceded the recognition of his part in the authorship of Script within a few days, thereby guaranteeing his share of any financial rewards accruing from the new arrangements.

Malone had no intention of doing any such thing. Intermediaries now pointed out that he was now dependent on Script teaching for his living, and that if he was troublesome the supply of Script textbooks could be cut off. John countered this by telling them that he had constructed his own shorthand system which he could teach if necessary. When Malone heard of this he began to plot a way to undermine John's shorthand prospects.

During this crisis in his life John talked to his older brother, Sam, about the treacherous behaviour of his co-partner. He felt that he could no longer be associated with such a dishonest individual. His brother was sympathetic, but anxious about his future. On the evening that the letter of resignation was posted John accompanied his brother to the railway station, and spoke of the three alternatives he had pondered on that day: he could continue his association with Script or return to a law office, or he could publish and teach a shorthand of his own invention. With some hesitation—for his brother had often referred to his shorthand research as 'John's mania'—he told how, a year before, he had developed an alphabet free from shading, position-writing, and other objectionable features.

His brother listened with greater interest than usual, stimulated by John's achievements of the previous months, and, when they reached the Exchange Station some minutes before the commuter's train, the discussion continued as they walked up and down the long platform. As John explained in detail the features of his system and the advantages which followed from his discovery, Sam grew enthusiastic and dramatically quoted Shakespeare:

> There is a tide in the affairs of men,
> Which taken at the flood, leads on to fortune;

Omitted, all the voyage of their life
Is bound in shallows, and in miseries;
And we must take the current when it serves,
Or lose our ventures.

Then, placing his hand on John's shoulder, Sam said: 'If you believe this system of yours is better than any other, you must publish it. That is a plain duty. But, my boy, it must not be published unless you are convinced that it is better. That would be wrong. It would not be right to publish it even if it is just as good as others. It must be better—decidedly better'.

That night John took from his trunk the package of his shorthand research papers which he had not touched since his sister's death. He tested the alphabet by writing several speeches and articles from the newspaper and quickly became excited by the fluency, easy curvature, and beauty of the writing. His confidence was not misplaced: the alphabet was superior to any he knew.

A few days later, on the 29th March, 1888, he copyrighted his alphabet in a broadsheet at the British Museum. Then he wrote his first textbook of Light-Line Phonography, called *Phonetic Hand-Writing,* and, with the assistance of a loan from Sam, published it on the 28th May, 1888—four days after his co-partnership contract with Malone expired.

Meanwhile Malone was desperately trying to engage the interests of potential shareholders in his projected new company. He attempted to get the backing of financiers in Nottingham and London—but he met great resistance. The businessmen were not prepared to risk capital to the management of one with such a poor record of achievement. In vain Malone expatiated on the profits to be obtained from branch schools and agencies throughout Britain, instancing the results of 'even a raw youth of 19 who had sold 1800 textbooks and enrolled 100 students within his first six months at Liverpool'. His plausible tongue won some support among some Glasgow professional men, disillusioned Sloan-Duployan teachers, and a few members of the Modern Shorthand Society. In all 58 gullible people provided Malone with £1,500 in exchange for the copyright of Script phonography.[3]

With the company organised and his financial position temporarily secure once more, Malone considered how he might embarrass John. He knew that it was his intention to teach, and possibly publish, a shorthand system of his own, and emboldened by the collective strength of his shareholders, he planned to obstruct his enterprise. He remembered that he still possessed two sheets of experimental alphabets which John had left with him during the summer of 1885 in illustration of the basic elements of a system to replace Sloan-Duployan shorthand. He decided to appropriate John's work, and on the 26th April, 1888, he registered at the British Museum, under the name 'Breviscript', the outline of a shorthand system containing John's ten principal consonants,[4] lifted bodily from John's own manuscript. Even the name 'Breviscript' was stolen from another person.[5]

In all probability Malone believed that by this registration he had obtained the legal possession of John's system, and if John was successful in his venture, he could claim the copyright and force him to pay an extortionate royalty. But Malone was ignorant of the great advances which John had made in his shorthand research since 1885. When he learned that John Robert Gregg had copyrighted a perfect alphabet some weeks earlier containing only two of the original characters[6] his rage knew no bounds. His next malicious act was to establish a branch school at Liverpool, to which his assistant, Mr Gallup, was sent immediately after the summer vacation with instructions 'to quash Gregg within three months'.

John's shorthand system was published in two parts: the first was a 28-page booklet, *Light-Line Phonetic Handwriting,* price one shilling, which contained the basic principles, and a second booklet of the same size, *The Reporter's Handbook,* gave advanced applications for those who wished to undertake more demanding work. That division of study was then accepted as the regular method of textbook exposition, but in John's case it was made necessary by his shortage of funds. Initially the money borrowed from his brother was sufficient to cover only the cost of the first booklet, and he was not able to pay for the second until he had received the fees of the pioneering Light-Line students.

The preface to *Light-Line Phonetic Handwriting* is of particular interest as it refers to certain ideas which were at that time preoccupying John's mind. It begins; 'A great and increasing demand for a simple, rapid, perfectly legible phonetic handwriting for general use has led to the invention of Light-Line Phonography. . . .' He hoped then, and continued to hope for the rest of his life, that he might see the day when his system would replace ordinary longhand writing for personal use, and thereby save an enormous quantity of time and effort. He also possessed an unshakable conviction that extreme simplicity of system was compatible with the most skilful shorthand writing. His preface ends with the words:

> The endeavour of the author has been to compile a system so simple as to be readily acquired by the humblest capacity, and those possessed of little leisure, and yet rapid enough to reproduce verbatim the fastest oratory. In presenting his work to the public, he asks for nothing beyond an impartial investigation, and with perfect confidence awaits the results.

It was remarkable assurance on the part of the 20-year-old author.

Initially there was great difficulty in presenting the new shorthand to the public, for John's resources were almost exhausted. But just as he had advertised Script on a tiny budget, so he found ways to bring Light-Line shorthand to the attention of the people of Liverpool. Principally it was by means of cheaply-produced handbills, leaflets, and posters. Economy could bring its own complications: his first low-cost printer distributed posters with the strange message: 'Gregg Shorthand. Words without angels'.

The first student of Light-Line was a youth of 18, Fred H. Spragg whom John taught from his own notes before the booklet was in print. The ease and speed with which Spragg gained skill in writing and reading the new shorthand gratified John, and encouraged him to invite a group of Script-writing acquaintances to study Light-Line. The first to accept was Mr J. J. Jakeman, who had formerly assisted with Script teaching, and the second was Mr J. Carlisle McCleery, an official in the Customs Department at Liverpool, who practised as a free-lance journalist. Mr McCleery set himself the challenge of reaching a hundred words a minute within one month—and accomplished that.

These men in turn spread the good news of this exciting invention among the local teachers and intellectuals. There was of course incredulity among those who had heard many times before of wonderful shorthand systems, which, on investigation failed to live up to expectations. Soon it was clear that if a teacher could be persuaded to spend an hour or two examining the system, that teacher was won over for Light-Line because Light-Line was so dramatically simple that it guaranteed quicker learning and easier teaching. Whereas the Pitman system was presented in some 200 rules and some 300 exceptions, there were only 30 simple rules in Light-Line; instead of zig-zag light and heavy geometric strokes located on various positions relative to the horizontal line, Light-Line offered elegant curves which flowed along the horizontal line of writing using the slope of ordinary longhand writing; in place of an elaborate word analysis to separate consonants from vowels, Light-Line joined consonants and vowels in their natural order.

When the intellectuals, shorthand enthusiasts, and historians discovered Light-Line, all but the entrenched bigots acknowledged that John had solved the problems which had pre-occupied the attentions of inventors for more than 2,000 years. Even Malone recognised the merits of Light-Line, and in an extremity of perversion he alleged that the system was a plagiarism of Script! To that absurdity the most succinct reply came from the distinguished Scandinavian shorthand historian, Olof Melin:[7] '[Light-Line] is so original both as to its general principles and its choice of symbols that the accusation of plagiarism must be absolutely rejected'.

The weeks which followed the publication of his system were among the most anxious of John's life up to that time. It was summer when few pupils were interested in studying, yet he had to maintain his office and set in motion publicity for his system. Then, unexpectedly, at the end of July a popular magazine called *Tit Bits* offered salvation, and as always John was ready to seize an opportunity. *Tit Bits* had printed an account of a Scottish court reporter by the name of Watts, who, it was claimed, had made the extraordinary record of writing legal matter in Pitman shorthand at the rate of 220 words a minute for 40 minutes. It was of course fantastic and merited an informed reply. John persuaded Mr McCleery to write to the editor one of his fluent humorous journalistic ripostes in which his happy experience of Light-Line was a prominent element. This letter started a furious exchange of views in the correspondence columns of *Tit Bits,* and by the time McCleery had drawn an admission of exaggeration from the original writer much interest had been aroused in the potential speed and fluency of Light-Line shorthand. Within a month John had received a thousand inquiries and his fees from the sale of textbooks and tuition brought him sufficient security to withstand the next assault, which was to come shortly afterwards.

Malone wanted to establish his branch schools throughout Britain. Having

32

quarrelled with his old associations, he sought new friends among the shorthand teachers of Edinburgh and London. His London contact was a Mr George C. Mares, who lived by shorthand teaching and journalism—following the failure of his own shorthand system, Rational Shorthand.[8] Mares had ability as a journalist, but was indolent, given to drink, and not too scrupulous about his loyalties providing a source of cash was forthcoming. He temporarily allied himself with Malone's projects, while continuing an extended correspondence with John concerning the nature of Light-Line and his experiences with Malone. Then one of John's Glasgow friends advised him that Mares was a director of Malone's new company and was acting as an 'undercover agent' and was passing John's letters to Malone. John was exceedingly annoyed. He cut off further communication and turned to his own advantage Mares' deception by quoting some of his warm praise for Light-Line in his next advertising leaflets. Mares and Malone then engineered the first stage of a legal action against John, alleging libel and slander.

While John was beset with the added financial burden of lawyer's fees in connection with the writ which had been issued, Malone's branch school at Liverpool opened with a massive advertising campaign for Script which specially attacked the Light-Line system and undercut John's tuition fees. At the Script school Mr Gallup was assisted by a young man called Boulton, whom he had recently introduced to the teaching profession in place of his normal occupation, which had been that of a waiter. However, the Script expectations were not fulfilled. The city people were conservative in their tastes and suspicious of yet another shorthand campaign, and both Gallup and John found themselves short of students. John fell considerably in arrears with his office rent and probably escaped eviction only because at that time there was little demand for commercial premises.

After some weeks of uncertainty John took a chance on a bold action: the office next door to his came vacant, and although in debt, he bargained with the astonished landlord for the second office. Then he painted upon the door 'Speed Rooms' and issued a prospectus in which he raised the rates for tuition, announcing 'This is the largest and most central school in Liverpool solely devoted to shorthand, and the only one having special classrooms where different rates of speed are maintained concurrently'. This resulted in a good number of people calling with inquiries. When some of them referred to the lower rates listed in earlier leaflets, or those charged by the Script school, John reduced the fees and obtained payment in advance. Soon he was busy once more—and fortunately the landlord did not call for rent for three months, having told the caretaker at the building that 'Gregg is a decent fellow, although a close-fisted Scotchman'.

By the end of December Malone's shareholders were alarmed at the losses being made at Liverpool and ordered Gallup to close the school. His assistant, Boulton, was unceremoniously dismissed, and in his fury he went to John and revealed the plans for legal action being prepared by Malone and Mares who expected him to be 'smashed by legal costs and expenses'. He admitted that he had allowed himself to be drawn into that scheme, and was responsible for inaccurate statements attributed to John, which the plotters depended upon for the success of their case. He then withdrew them, and left John with a signed apology.

Thus another crisis passed. John continued to labour enormously hard. Throughout the day he tramped about the schools speaking to teachers of the advantages of Light-Line, and from six to ten o'clock each night he taught at his school. The great majority of his pupils wanted to obtain only a minimum degree of proficiency for commercial work, but there were occasional enthusiasts whose performance gave promise of distinguished future achievements. One such person was Edward Deason, a newspaper reporter in his late twenties, who had worked in America without shorthand (using an abbreviated longhand of his own devising.) He came during the slack days of August when John could give him a greater portion of his time than usual. Deason displayed a remarkable talent for shorthand writing, and was anxious to achieve a verbatim writing ability as quickly as possible. Within a few weeks he was matching Spragg in taking commercial material at speeds far beyond those of the other students.

By the spring of 1889 the Script Phonography Company shareholders were growing restless because the programme of expansion and profit-making promised to them had not materialised. In fact, few pupils were coming to Malone for tuition, and the boasts contained in his advertising booklet *Science Victorious* rang hollow now that half the number of teachers who gave testimonials for Script had abandoned that system in favour of Light-Line shorthand. Worse still, the agents who were to organise classes and to whip up sales of text-books developed a justifiable suspicion of Malone's business methods, and one by one they dropped their agencies: first, the well-established Cranston and Tyndale at Edinburgh, then the London agents George C. Mares and Oliver McEwan upon whom Malone was relying for sales and publicity. In the event the only publicity he got was exceedingly bad. Both men were free-lance jounalists and did not hesitate to explain in print why they had given up Script. The March issue of *The Reporter's Magazine* printed an interview with McEwan which graphically illustrated the deficiencies of the system which he was no longer prepared to teach.[9] On the other hand, Light-Line started to receive favourable reviews in the press of Britain and foreign countries as distant as South Africa, Canada, America, New Zealand and Australia.

To coincide with an effort to attract more shareholders, Malone instituted another legal suit against John, comfortable in the knowledge that even if it failed his company would be responsible for the expenses, while John, who had no such subsidy, would have to finance his own defence and was likely to be ruined in the process.

For months John had been building up a steady succession of expanding evening classes, and now felt that he could safely leave them in charge of his assistant, Mr J. J. Jakeman, while he started classes in Manchester, another great industrial city 35 miles away. That class was warmly supported and brought John various useful contacts and a personal friend from among his students, a young married man, Robert Bowle.[10] Bowle proceeded to apply much of his spare time to furthering the cause of Light-Line shorthand not only in Manchester but throughout Southern England. He sent advertising literature to the local colleges and schools, and YMCA institutes at Bristol and London, and offered to run classes for teachers free of charge. More often than not his offers were refused — the English educational establishments were conservative and the response usually was similar to that received from the London YMCA educational officer who declined with the words: 'Pitman's shorthand is unanimously declared to be the best system'. Bowle was more easily disheartened than John, and his salesmanship was not particularly effective, yet John was grateful for his generous efforts, and when in the Autumn he opened a branch school at Manchester, he employed Bowle as his assistant evening teacher.

John believed that success would come principally through his own efforts and the inherent quality of his system, and he had the satisfaction of seeing slow and regular progress. In April, 1889, he wrote to his brother Jared: 'Rome was not built in a day, and my faith in the ultimate success of my cause has never been shaken by any adverse circumstances'.

During the year he printed his booklets in a fifth edition, and encouraged Spragg and Deason in their rapidly increasing skills. By May, Spragg was writing 180 words per minute and Deason 200 words per minute on literary matter, for several minutes at a time. Such fluency was exceedingly rare even among reporters of many years experience in other systems. From time to time John was greatly cheered by the success of self-taught Light-Line students, particularly those intellectuals who had tried one shorthand system after another in an effort to discover one which could live up to the promised expectations. An example of such was the letter he received from a Dr Kleiner, of Eccles (Lancashire), who wrote on the 18th July, 1889:

Dear Sir,
About three months since I purchase your two small text books of Light-Line Phonograpy. I have learned the system and have since taught my son, who is but 8 years of age, and I am glad to say he took up the principles of your system with the greatest of ease and is now, after having had about 90 hours study and practice, able to write at the rate of 50 words a minute, both English and German and he never finds any difficulty in reading what he has written.
I feel obliged to let you know the results I obtained with your system as to the ease with which it can be acquired, and its legibility stands ahead of any other system I have studied.

Yours truly
E. D. Kleiner, Ph.D.

Malone, sheltering under the collective anonymity and the financial strength of the Script Phonography Company, set in motion on the 26th July, 1889, what was to be a long-drawn-out legal action against John, alleging that his Light-Line shorthand infringed the copyright of Script Phonography. The claims were absurd to any one informed on the subject: nevertheless, the legal

35

papers submitted to the High Court of Justice at London were voluminous and elaborate and required the extensive—and expensive—services of expert lawyers to make adequate reply. The action was planned in two stages: first, an Interim Injunction was sought, whereby the court could order an immediate stop to the alleged offence, pending a hearing of the complaint; second, a trial at a later date, during which the case could be argued in court. With calculated malice Malone started the proceedings for the Interim Injunction[11] shortly before the courts closed for the summer 'long vacation', and if it had been granted, it would have prevented John doing any business for two months—which would have been disastrous. It was clearly Malone's intention to ruin him by this legal manoeuvre. Moreover, Malone had very good reasons for not wishing to proceed to a trial, for that would certainly expose his own dishonesty.

To make it more difficult for John to defend himself, the writ was issued on a Monday and the written replies to the allegations had to be delivered for the following Thursday. Fortunately, John acted swiftly. He consulted a sympathetic lawyer and arrangements were made for his representation at London, and a week's postponement of the hearing was obtained. During this time John worked night and day to gather evidence to answer the charges being made against him.

Malone, in addition to his own lengthy Statement of Complaint, had obtained numerous sworn depositions from those who were reputed to be authorities in shorthand matters, and others connected with the Script company in Glasgow. In his own statement, and several of the others too, all references to John's share in the construction of Script were omitted, to make it appear that the invention was solely the work of one individual.[12] Malone also submitted documents which purported to give details of an internal inquiry by the directors of the first Script company concerning the circumstances of John's resignation, but that document was, in fact, a later invention filled with inaccuracies, intended to mislead the judge during the court hearing. Malone's deposition was perjured, and so inconsistent and charged with deliberate distortions that it is a wonder that he supposed that it might ever be upheld in a court of law.

He begins the history of his relations with John with the astonishing statement that: 'John Robert Gregg. . . came to me at my shorthand institute at 192 Hope Street, Glasgow, and I taught him the system he was then studying, and subsequently, taught him Script Phonography'. The rest of his account was equally untrue. Among other things, he claimed that Light-Line shorthand had plagiarised the Script consonants and vowels and paraphrased the language of his textbooks, and imitated his rules; and, by strained comparisons, attempted to show that the Script system could be interpreted as possessing Light-Line shorthand's finest qualities, such as its blended consonants and its single-thickness characters.

An examination of the two systems clearly shows that Light-Line uses the same character for only 'F' and 'V', and these signs were common to many other shorthand systems long before Script. The vowels are different. In fact,

Malone's own evidence disproves his claims so fully that it is surprising that he did not realise that it could not fool any legal mind.

To John's relief the judge at the High Court refused to grant the Interim Injunction—he asked only that a record be kept of the sales of Light-Line textbooks until the time of the trial, expected to be held towards the end of the year. This was a great disappointment for Malone, who in his customary manner had freely used other people's money and had run up large legal expenses. His London lawyer had engaged the services of a leading advocate, Cousins Hardy, Q.C. to handle the case at court; and, feeling uncertain of Malone's chances, had taken costly Counsel's Opinion[13] from a Mr Church, who had advised that the evidence put before him would not entitle the Script Company to an injunction.

Early in the Autumn of 1889 John opened a branch school at Manchester. His evening classes there had been so well attended and the students so willing to recommend others that he had resolved to increase the opportunities for the study of Light-Line in that thriving industrial and commercial city. He rented a fine centrally located office on the corner of Market and Corporation Streets, and in high spirits began a vigorous advertising campaign to acquaint the people of Manchester that his new school was ready to receive them. But the public response was slow and the number of students who did enrol was not in proportion to his expenditure of energy and money. John was particularly disappointed by the absence of those friends and relatives of the evening class students whom he was assured would support the day school. Nevertheless, he was confident that business would improve, and he felt no serious financial anxiety because the Liverpool school was doing well, and it had been left to the management of an honest and conscientious teacher.

Edward Deason was now persuaded to give a 'puff' to Light-Line shorthand and the Manchester school by demonstrating his skill as an exponent of the system in public. He had by now developed a fluency and expertise which at least matched the best performance which had been witnessed by reliable observers in England at that time.

In the 1880s people throughout the English-speaking world conducted their business in the law courts and on political platforms with greater deliberation than at present, so that there was little call for fast shorthand writing. Although records of speed were often claimed by the competing systems, the tests were generally held in private among shorthand society members. Now John organised one of the rare public performances.

On the evening of 11th October 1889, persons interested in shorthand were invited to the Public Hall at Salford, two miles from Manchester, where they could dictate matter of their own choice to Edward Deason. It must have been a somewhat anxious night for John, for while he had absolute confidence in Light-Line shorthand, he could not be so entirely happy about Deason, who was moody, and at times unreliable. Although charged with great drive and ambition, he did not share John's educational ideals and deep love of shorthand for its own sake. Shorthand, in Deason's opinion, was a means to a rapid advancement and high salary. That night, however, Deason gave a magnificent display of rapid writing and fluent reading, culminating in the taking of dictation on unseen theological matter, chosen and read by a leading Pitman teacher, at the speed of 200 words per minute for 6 minutes and 45 seconds, and read back without a single error. The astonished teacher, Mr J. M. Pontefract, and several other well-qualified teachers signed a statement that they had witnessed the demonstration which surpassed in speed and accuracy anything of which they had knowledge.

Slowly the Manchester school gained students, but to John's dismay the Liverpool business simultaneously declined. John had been depending upon the receipts from the Liverpool school to finance the first few months at Manchester, until the tuition fees and textbook sales would balance the expenses. By Christmas John's funds were exhausted. He decided to return to Liverpool to rebuild his school there, and made over the Manchester branch to another Light-Line teacher on the understanding that he would pay two months' rent owing on the office.

John's letters to Bowle record the struggle he had during the next few months, when as he put it, 'Our enemies, particularly the Scriptites, are howling and growling'. Without his administrative supervision and personal teaching, the morale of the assistants and the standards of the students had dropped-off seriously. But, by degrees, he recovered what had been lost— always under the strain of worrying about the printer's bills, the legal costs, and the business overheads. Just as he was beginning to escape from debt he learned that the teacher left in charge at Manchester had absconded with his pockets full of advance fees taken from students to whom he had fraudulently guaranteed unreasonable attainments—leaving John to pay the printer for the dishonest advertising literature, and four months of office rent!

On the 24th March 1890 he wrote to Bowle:

> You can't imagine how busy I am—teaching from morning to night without intermission. It is very rarely indeed that I have a moment to myself. Since my return from Manchester I have set myself steadily to work to rebuild my connection again and repair the mischief done by my absence in Manchester. I have made friends of my pupils by giving them good tuition—turning them out practical writers—and at last I am getting clear of my difficulties and am doing good business. I can now confidently rely upon the recommendations of my pupils. The amount of advertising I do infinitesimal. But for the merit—the decided and palpable merit—of the system, I could never have pulled my business together again, and merit must prevail in the end, steadily pushed.

He also advised Bowle that their mutual friend, Fred Spragg, who had gone to work for the Salvation Army in London, was temporarily back in Liverpool, 'and that he would take care of that giddy young man and give him some hints, and fully impress upon him the importance of a London public test.[14] It is one of my bricks in the building of my scheme for the future'. Unfortunately he was to be disappointed by Spragg: that young man was a weak and self-indulgent person, who would never apply his considerable ability except under the direct pressure of some one like John.

On the 24th April, 1890, John wrote to Bowle:

Well I have some news for you this time—something that will make you smile and smile. The Script action has been *Dismissed with Costs.* Fetch out the band and kiss the baby—and generally speaking do reckless things. I think I may pass on without comment—well, no, I must add that my solicitors are most solicitous as to the financial condition of the Script Company. Bless you, they're very nice men are solicitors!

Malone was now in deep trouble with his directors. Typically he attempted to blame his lawyers for the result of the action—they had not followed his instructions, he claimed. In this, as in so much else, he misrepresented the facts.[15]

There was much work ahead of John to recover from the heavy legal expenses.[16] He instituted another campaign to promote interest in his system and carried it through by a huge personal correspondence and a great deal of visiting at the schools and institutions within his reach. He had the satisfaction of receiving many letters of thanks and appreciation from an ever-widening geographical area. The eminent French shorthand authority, Jean P. A. Martin, of Lyons, (whose own adaption of the Duployan system John had studied some years before) wrote in approval:

I can but think well of a system which embodies all the ideas defended by me time and again. . . . . I have no doubt it will soon produce reporters, and their notes will be of value to shorthand scientists. I shall watch your progress with great interest . . . . I look upon your system as a very valuable experiment. Your principles are scientific, and science knows no borders, no nationalities, it is human'.

The first reporter to make a practical use of Light-Line was George G. Armstrong of Liverpool, in 1891 a very young man starting upon a life which was to bring him a distinguished place in newspaper history.[17] Before long he was writing to the inventor:

You may rely upon my consistent advocacy of the merits of your system, among my confrères as a reporting medium. It appears to me to be unapproached for legibility, ease and rapidity of execution and facility of acquisition. I never felt the slightest doubt since becoming a reporter as to the wisdom of my choice of shorthand'.

Interest in Light-Line shorthand was growing in America, Canada, and South Africa, and it was usually the result of highly favourable newspaper and magazine reviews of the system written both by amateur shorthand enthusiasts and professional journalists. The commercial prospects for those willing to teach the system were also beginning to be appreciated throughout the British colonies. In this connection John received a call from a Mr George Watson, who had just retired as an officer of the Salvation Army at London, and was about to emigrate to Canada. He told John that until recently he had been a writer of Pitman shorthand, but had been converted to Light-Line shorthand by

Spragg, who had lodged at the same house, and he asked John's opinion of his chances to make a living from teaching the system in Toronto. He was warmly encouraged, and appointed an agent for the sale of Light-Line textbooks in Canada.

At Glasgow, Malone realised that he had exhausted the patience and gold of his shareholders and planned to move to London, where his reputation was little known, and there was an abundance of speculators in risky ventures. His going was hastened by the threat to wind-up the company from a Mr Miller, a lawyer and director, who declared that, 'In his opinion it was little better than a fraud'.[18] At London Malone persuaded a number of school teachers to subscribe the sum of £400 to the Script Company to offset a deficiency which had been discovered in the books, and he was temporarily enabled to continue his operations.[19] He next published another edition of the Script textbook in which he blatantly stole John Robert Gregg's character for 'S',[20] and also stole his description of 'blended consonants'—but the unique advantages given by John's blended consonants were not accessible to him.

Light-Line shorthand was materially assisted in 1892 by the publicity which resulted from a controversy which raged for five months in the popular weekly magazine *The Bazaar, Exchange & Mart.* On the 15th January, a middle-aged man, Mr D. Denning, recommended Light-Line to young people proposing to study shorthand, and praised it as wonderfully easy to learn by comparison with the older systems. Writers of other systems hurried to scoff at the advice, and this in turn brought a fierce defence from Light-Line teachers. Among these was the respected Edinburgh teacher Frederick Tyndall who had tried all the other systems without satisfaction. He told of his experiment of teaching Light-Line to the eleven-to-thirteen-year-old children at the grade school at Portobello, and of results after three months which were equal to those expected normally after a full year of instruction with other systems.

John received many hundreds of inquiries for literature describing his shorthand and a goodly number of new students for his classes and correspondence courses. The editor closed the correspondence in his paper with these remarks:

The real point at issue, in a nutshell, is: 'Is Light-Line a workable system?' Up to the present the weight of evidence is very much in its favour; for not only has it been pretty conclusively shown to be a practical one but also that it has fewer complications, and is thus more easily acquired than the older systems formed upon geometric principles.

By May John wrote to a friend that he 'was swamped with work'. In addition to his teaching he had to reply to a voluminous mail personally. Among his inquiries, one came from a Mr A. St. Clair Humphrys, a 31-year-old teacher who had been impressed by the experience of others in his profession who had experimented with Light-Line. He began teaching it at Newcastle-on-Tyne. The progress of his students led him to an extensive exchange of notes with John, and subsequently he became an agent for Light-Line in Northern England, and a close friendship developed between the two men.

Other teachers reported successful evening classes for young men at the YMCA centres at Bristol, Cardiff, and London, and from Exeter came news of the fine examination results from schoolchildren in classes organised by G. Ridsdale Blake, a respected commercial educator. In May 1892, Mr Ridsdale Blake established *The Light-Line Magazine* which consisted of twelve pages of articles written in shorthand. From the second issue John gave his support, and wrote all the outlines for the magazine, which was produced monthly by the lithographic process. John expanded *The Light-Line Magazine* by including news of shorthand from around the world, in English print, as well as articles in shorthand. Although at first the circulation was small, it proved to be a valuable means of providing information and acted as a cohesive force among the pioneer teachers and the widely-separated enthusiasts for the new system.

An interesting feature is that from the very beginning both the editor and John encouraged women and girls to undertake the study of shorthand. Although at that time few British commercial offices had admitted either lady clerks or typewriters, both men recognised that a major social change was about to take place, similar to that which was then occurring in America. Their recommendations were picked up in the magazine *The Queen* where it provoked discussion concerning the suitability of shorthand and typewriting training for young women. One of John's earliest pupils, Miss A. E. Sidley, who had risen to become the manager of the Tuition Department[21] of the Bar-Lock typewriter Company at Liverpool, wrote an account of her experiences to *The Queen:*[22]

I have been teaching typewriting and Light-Line phonography for the past three years, and during that time a great number of pupils, ranging in age from twelve to sixty years, have passed through my hands, and to all of them Light-Line has proved a boon . . . . Until within the last few years the art of shorthand writing has been practised almost exclusively by men, and women have been quite content to have it so, as very few of those who had to earn their living had either the time or money to spend twelve to fifteen months in learning it. . . . But since Light-Line has come before the public, the women shorthand writers of England bid fair to exceed the men, as it is a system peculiarly adapted to a lady's style of handwriting.

At the beginning of 1893 Ridsdale Blake reported to John that he had financial problems and could no longer afford to maintain *The Light-Line Magazine.* John then took responsibility for the magazine, renaming it *The Light-Liner.* He extended its range by obtaining articles from his friends and acquaintances with journalistic skills. He made a special point of printing many references to those who had improved their fortune by personal effort— for it was now an established custom with John to cultivate in others a confidence that they were able to achieve their ambitions through personal effort and well-organised self-education, and that Shorthand offered the very best start upon that progress.

The first issue of his own magazine, *The Light-Liner,* was published in

February. The editorial work and the supervision of production added yet another labour to a young man working extremely long hours already; nevertheless, John found the strength to cope, and was happy to have scope for his own journalistic skills. Unfortunately the circulation was too small to attract paid advertising, and the price— kept at three pence to encourage the young readers—scarcely reduced the considerable loss on each issue. John was content to subsidise it, for interest in his system was growing day by day and he anticipated an acceleration in the adoption of Light-Line shorthand throughout the country.

Then he was struck by an appalling misfortune: he suddenly became deaf in his 'good' ear! For several weeks he was stone-deaf. He could not teach, nor supervise others in his little school nor continue his 'Missionary work' among the teachers and shorthand-writers. His income dropped dramatically as his pupils fell off and the sale of textbooks diminished. Under such circumstances many people have given way to despair; John Robert Gregg did not. What he did was seek the best medical advice, and throw the greater part of his energy into writing and editorial work for the *Light-Liner.*

He gathered articles on the study and practice of shorthand from other journals; persuaded his acquaintances to send in contributions of interest to the learners; prepared helpful comments upon the shorthand given in the magazine (all of which he wrote himself with the unmanageable, greasy, lithographic ink), and kept up a steady flow of information about the successes of those attending the schools run by Watson in Canada, Baines in Australia, Humphrys in Newcastle, Tyndale in Edinburgh, and the newest of all, at London, recently opened by a Miss Amy Johnson.

John's second ear gradually responded to treatment. By early May he felt able to undertake a campaign to win Light-Line writers in Northern Ireland, and in the company of A. Ashborne Taylor, his assistant at Liverpool, he went to Belfast to use that city as a base from which to travel to the towns in a wide radius. In the course of three weeks he gave nine public lectures to large audiences and attracted five favourable reviews of some length in the press. Even those papers which hesitated to acknowledge the superiority of the Light-Line system could not ignore him. The *Ulster Echo,* after declining to offer any assessment of the comparative merits of Light-Line shorthand observed that: 'Mr Gregg is pushing his system with tact and energy. We wish all success in his efforts after reform in shorthand which has now become a desideratum'. The Pitman and Sloan pundits were highly alarmed, and on one occasion there was an attempt to disturb one of his public meetings.

The campaign, which was undoubtedly a success, resulted in the sale of more than a thousand textbooks and the establishment of an ambience of warm interest which could be cultivated by a local agent. Such a person presented himself when a Mr P. Murray was converted to Light-Line at one of John's public meetings. Mr Murray took some lessons from John at Belfast, then continued by himself until he had mastered the system. He then opened a school of shorthand at Belfast. Within a few months he distinguished himself by obtaining the only first-class certificate at 140 words a minute in shorthand which was awarded in the year by the Royal Society of Arts in Ireland.

Back in Liverpool John was beginning to regain business when he was faced with another potential disaster: His North American agent, Frank Rutherford of Boston, motivated by greed and encouraged by his own success, wrote that he was going to publish the Light-Line textbook in America, and generously offered to allow John 'a small commission'. This was an extremely worrying matter for John because he had always intended to extend his activities to America. If Rutherford were to publish his shorthand system there, he would lose the copyright[23] and all the advantages which were connected with it. The only course which lay open to him was to protect his interest by depositing as soon as possible an outline of his system at the Library of Congress at Washington. He did not have the means to do it personally, but he remembered the offer of friendly assistance made by a loyal enthusiast, Mr James B. Burrows, who had settled in Chicago. Through his agency a synopsis of his system, in the form of a broadsheet, *Gregg's System of Shorthand,*[24] was lodged with the Library of Congress.

Meanwhile John kept up a correspondence with Rutherford concerning the possibilities of a major American campaign to win the country over to his shorthand.

It had become clear to John that he would have to travel to America to conduct such a campaign personally and to publish his textbook there, and it seemed necessary to involve Rutherford as an associate in that venture. John's friend, St Clair Humphrys, warned him there would be difficulties, for he knew Rutherford as a self-seeking adventurer who had taken refuge in America following some serious financial transgressions in England. However, he did possess one redeeming quality which was of practical significance for John's plans: he was a genuine enthusiast for his shorthand, and according to his own account, he had a flourishing school at Boston from which the educational programme could be waged.

John immediately made preparations for his American travel. He revised his textbook in the light of five years' teaching and writing, and he entered into a temporary partnership agreement with St Clair Humphrys, whereby he would run the publishing business and the agency supervision in his absence. The greatest problem was to raise sufficient money. Reluctantly he acknowledged that his only realisable asset was the Liverpool school. He then sold a major interest in that school to a Mr Whitford, a shorthand amateur who was looking for a new investment because his shipping business had been seriously affected by the business depression which was then affecting the country.

In the second week of August 1893, John had settled his affairs sufficiently to allow him to travel. After a brief visit to his family at Glasgow, he joined a ship full of emigrants, carrying with him $130 to start him on a crusade for Gregg Shorthand in the New World.

CHAPTER NOTES

1. February 24, 1888.
2. March 24, 1888.
3. The new company, 'Script Phonography Company Limited' was incorporated June 14, 1888.
4. P B T D N M R L K G
5. It was the name given to the system which a Mr Browne described in *The Journalist,* January 28, 1887.
6. The 'T' and 'D'.
7. Author of *History of Shorthand* (Stenografiens historie), Stockholm, 1927.
8. *Rational Shorthand,* London, 1885.
9. No person, other than J.R.G, ever ran a successful Script shorthand school.
10. The 'L' in Bowle was suppressed in pronunciation.
11. Intended to prevent John from selling or teaching 'Lightline Shorthand.
12. Two of those who gave depositions, Webster and Mares, were in later years to seek J R G's forgiveness for allowing falsified statements to be used against him.
13. Counsel's Opinion: a British legal specialist's advice.
14. Comparable to Deason's performance at Salford.
15. The documents are still in existence, in the Gregg Archives. They reached Mr Gregg through the agency of George C. Mares, who was sorry for the wrong he had done years before.
16. Malone had incurred even greater legal expenses. He did not lodge the 'Statement of Claim' within the prescribed period of time set by the court. The directors of the Script Phonography Company were advised by their counsel that they could not expect to win the case against John. Undoubtedly they ordered Malone not to proceed with further legal action.
17. George Gilbert Armstrong, 1870-1945, Editor and Chairman of *Daily News* (Manchester).
18. Letter, Mr McKay (a former teacher of Script Phonography) to J R G
19. Among the shareholders who lost money to Malone was the future Prime Minister of Britain, Bonar Law.
20. This outline had never previously been used for this purpose in any shorthand.
21. All the typewriter companies found it necessary to offer training to users of their machines, at that time.
22. October 15, 1892.
23. There was then no comprehensive International Copyright agreement.
24. The broadsheet was registered July 14, 1893. A system of shorthand with the title 'Lightline' had already been registered in America, so from this time, John Robert Gregg's system was known by his own name.

Chapter Three To America—with Confidence and Conviction

The £4 which John had paid for his passage on the *Nestorian* entitled him to few comforts during the three weeks slow rolling travel towards Boston. However, the tedium of the journey was somewhat relieved by the friendship which he made with two Scotchmen, Girvan and Mackie, who hoped to improve their fortunes across the sea. Having won them over to the cultural and economic benefits of shorthand, he tutored them daily in Gregg Shorthand.[1] By the time they reached America, they had sufficiently mastered the system to feel confident about teaching it, and proceeded to Fitchburg, Massachusetts, where they started the first Gregg Shorthand class for adults in America.[2]

Rutherford had been wired that John was aboard the *Nestorian* which was due to dock on the 22nd August. His feelings must have been mixed, because he had not seriously expected John to travel to America, and moreover he had to abandon his dream of affluence to be acquired through a monopoly in the sale of Gregg Shorthand textbooks in America. Worse, his pretence of being a successful school proprietor was shortly to be exposed as false. In truth, he had only a handful of private pupils, and one children's shorthand class at a charity institution. Nevertheless, he could look forward to the prospect of joining forces with another shorthand enthusiast in the propaganda and missionary work on behalf of a shorthand system for which he had a genuine admiration.

When he went to meet the ship he took with him a recent acquaintance, Louis Pfeiffer, an ambitious youth of seventeen who had just completed a two-year commercial course and was considering embarking upon a teaching career. A friend of Pfeiffer's father had recommended that he speak with Rutherford who was the representative for the new British shorthand which had recently received some publicity in one of the leading shorthand journals, *The Phonographic World.* Pfeiffer met Rutherford, but was repulsed by his opinionated, aggressive manner; but, being of a gregarious disposition, he was very willing to make the acquaintance of a shorthand inventor about whom he had read.

They had a considerable wait before John reached the pier because the immigration officials, noting that he had left from Glasgow, although all his documents were from Liverpool, closely questioned him about the 130 dollars he carried—it being so much more than his poverty-stricken fellow travellers possessed. At length they were satisfied that his money was lawfully acquired and released him to the pier to meet two people who were to be closely associated with his life for the next eighteen months.

The weather was exceedingly hot, and as soon as introductions were made, Rutherford suggested that they indulge in a 'soda'. John, who had never heard of this trans-Atlantic delight, was mystified until they reached the nearest drugstore—he had previously associated the word with whisky only. John then

JOHN R. GREGG, AGED 34

inquired about the prospects for shorthand in Boston. He was told that things were more than difficult: it was the year of the 'Great Panic', the economic depression during which business confidence was undermined, and all the commentators agreed that America was experiencing its worst year since the Civil War. Boston was suffering severely, and at the City Hall soup was being served to long lines of hungry people. Commercial life was sluggish and most of the stenographers were unemployed. There could be no worse time to start a campaign for a new shorthand system!

Louis Pfeiffer immediately liked John for his polite manner and his quiet speech, and the confidence he had in his system. He willingly accepted a gift of the first textbook and promised to examine it carefully, and to report his opinion at a later date. They then took John to visit Rutherford's 'school', which was revealed as a desk in a large office[3] on Milk Street, where space was subrented to seven or eight other people by the official occupant, a German farmer's agent called Strout. Here, on the desk slides, Rutherford offered shorthand and typewriting tuition to his very few pupils. Arrangements were soon made to install another roll-top desk at the cost of 12 dollars per month.

In the interests of economy John temporarily joined Rutherford at his inexpensive lodgings, which he rented from a doctor friend of Pfeiffer's father, in 'Chinatown'.[4] Then, from the communal office he planned a campaign for advertising Gregg shorthand and printing the revised textbook. It was his intention to establish classes in schools and other educational institutions with

46

the expectation that they would be self-perpetuating and provide a reasonable income from the sale of textbooks; however, he was also keen to encourage inquiries for private tuition, by mail and in person. Almost immediately he had a large poster printed in bold type which read:

AT LAST
Gregg's Shorthand[5]
Can be acquired in as many weeks as other systems require months. No more studying session after session and year after year. Unlimited tuition until a specified speed is attained. No failures.

These he had posted up all round Harvard University. Then he inserted small advertisements in the local papers offering mail tuition in Gregg shorthand at '10 lessons for $1.75, cash in advance'.

About a week after he had arrived in Boston, Louis Pfeiffer presented himself at John's desk and demanded: 'Dictate a letter to me. I will write in Gregg shorthand!' He proved that he could take and read back satisfactorily. He had absorbed the contents of the first book and was ready to continue with the more advanced textbook. John recognised that in Pfeiffer he had found a good ally, and henceforth included him in his programme of action. The most pressing matter was to get an American edition of the textbook printed and copyrighted. The cost was unexpectedly high, and initially John could afford to publish only *'Gregg's Shorthand Part one: the Elements.*[6] By comparison with the earlier English editions, this 36-page booklet contained a good deal more letterpress explanation, and two small modifications were made to the alphabet: the signs for 'NG' and 'NK' were sloped downwards, instead of lying horizontal. Also included were various abbreviations for common words which had been tried and tested in the *Lightliner* magazine.

Louis Pfeiffer quickly developed a high regard for John; they got on exceedingly well together for both had a similar sense of humour and loved to exchange stories of their adventures and experiences. Pfeiffer made himself most useful to John by undertaking numerous small commissions in connection with the printing of the new textbook. Later, he accompanied him on his visits to public schools where they held meetings with groups of teachers who might be persuaded to consider the advantages of studying, and subsequently teaching, Gregg shorthand. Pfeiffer introduced John to his family circle, and he became a welcome weekend guest at their summer home at Bedford[7] and at the medical institute which his father supervised on Massachusetts Avenue in Boston.

Dr Pfeiffer strongly disapproved of Boston as a base-camp for John's shorthand campaign. He considered that the people were too conservative in their tastes, and unlikely to respond as John hoped. He urged him to move to bustling, expanding Chicago, where business was less depressed and the population was better disposed to try whatever was new. But John had set things in motion in Boston and felt himself bound to remain there for some time. Even though he had the greatest reservations about his cooperation with Rutherford, he believed that because of their poverty they were likely to have better prospects if they joined forces. He entered into an agreement to share expenses and profits with Rutherford for a period of three years from the 28th August, 1893. It was to prove a most unhappy partnership.

A large number of shorthand systems were offered in America in the 1890s, but most of them were variations of the parent system of Sir Isaac Pitman. The especially favoured Pitmanic system was that of Ben Pitman, Sir Isaac's brother, which claimed more than 34%[8] of the shorthand market. All these, and the one non-Pitmanic system, Cross Eclectic,[9] were very much more difficult to acquire than Gregg shorthand, and few of the teachers were happy with them. John supposed that the Boston teachers would appreciate the simplicity of his own shorthand and that it would quickly win them over through its intrinsic merit.

On the 21st October, 1893, John wrote to Humphrys:

'I write in joyous spirit. The printer is pushing on with the second book;[10] I managed to scrape together enough to satisfy him. But I have better news than that. I think I told you that I was to lecture to an audience of teachers. The lecture was fairly successful as a class of 10 enrolled at $5 each for a course of 12 lessons. That is what enabled me to meet the printer. I think I also told you that I was sending out an inkpress *Lightline* to all the headmasters and members of the school board. A member[11] has replied and it turns out, for a few years he has been using his influence to get shorthand introduced into the curriculum of study, but the systems hitherto tried have proved failures, and his wish has been defeated. He was impressed by Lightline. He has decided to learn the system himself in order to test it in practice. He will devote two hours a day to the study; if he finds it a success, he will go to his colleagues, tell them his experiences and suggest its adoption in the Normal colleges for teachers so that the teachers will be qualified to teach and thus to have it adopted in every school.

Let me take breath; well, this happened a couple of hours ago and I am anxious to let you see a glorious future there is in store for us here. It must influence us in England—throughout the whole world in fact. If Boston, educated, enlightened, cultured Boston leads the van with Lightline. Of course I know that 'there is many a slip between cup and lip' but the fact that we have had such a success already is a good omen for the future.

Pupils began to respond to his advertisements for both private tuition and correspondence courses, and he was able to start the YMCA classes, and one grammar school[12] did adopt the system, but the numbers of 50-cent booklets sold did not meet his expectations and scarcely offset the costs of advertising and the living expenses of two people.

Those who took instruction from John were more than pleased with their progress. One of his pupils, Miss Stewart, was the daughter of the superintendent of the philanthropic Boys' Institute of Industry,[13] and through her John obtained two evenings' teaching (at $1 per evening of three hours instruction). At almost the same time a young woman, Miss Smith from Salem, enrolled for twelve lessons, and conscientiously cycled to his office each Saturday

*Mr Gregg's first shorthand class in America, at the Boys' Institute of
Industry, Boston, Massachusetts, 1893*

afternoon for private tuition. At the end of the course she revealed that she was a teacher of Pitman shorthand working for the Salem Commercial School. The proprietor, Miss Emma Tibbetts, had asked her to test Gregg shorthand, and learn if it was more suitable than Pitman for the college. Miss E. L. Smith, convinced by her personal experience, was the first American teacher to be converted to Gregg shorthand teaching from another system.[14]

From England John received Humphrys' weekly letters keeping him in touch with the news from the Gregg shorthand agents at Liverpool, Edinburgh, London and Manchester. Much of it was disquieting: in particular, Mr Whitford was proving to be belligerent, unreasonable and grasping. He had little skill in teaching or organising teachers, and John's former assistant, Taylor, was finding it almost impossible to work with him. Whitford, having been disappointed in his expectations of large profits, was now attempting to break his contract whereby he was to pay John £250 in instalments. He now claimed that he had been left insufficient textbooks and the expenses of the Liverpool school were too high. The complaints were intended to give a semblance of justification to his impending action. Fortunately, Humphrys was about to supply him with a quantity of the newly revised textbook— published simultaneously in America and England to meet the copyright laws. The alleged excessive expenses Whitford dealt with in his own way by abandoning the rooms at 62 Dale Street, Liverpool, without paying the landlord!

John wrote to Humphrys on the 13th November, 1893: 'There is no blinking the fact that Whitford is dangerous. Our position to him is one of great gravity.' Nevertheless, he wrote to Whitford in a conciliating tone likely to turn his mind from possible litigation. To Humphrys he confided: 'Whitford knows that I have little or no money, am at a distance, and if he rushed his action he might get hold of the system and force my hand so that I would grant him whatever he asks'.

Humphrys was advised of developments in Boston and reassured that Rutherford would not get hold of the copyright which he, too, coveted.

> No, I have no intention of parting with any share in my American copyright, and I mean to reserve New York for myself. I have no intention of planting Rutherford there. As a matter of fact I can not rely on Rutherford too much. As you always insisted, he is, I regret to say, too much inclined to take the reins out of my hands. He is enthusiastic, energetic, and has ability, but not too much good judgement or tact. I say this in order that you may know that I am not placing too much confidence in him.

At the *Silver Jubilee convention of Gregg Shorthand* in 1913, John Robert Gregg reminisced of his first Christmas in the States:[15]

> No Christmas that I have ever had in my life will stick in my memory like that first Christmas day in Boston in 1893. As Christmas approached business dwindled to the vanishing point—you all know how students drop off at that time of the year. Now,

Christmas is the day of days in the old country, and Rutherford and I determined that we were going to do the best we could to have one good Christmas dinner. We summed up our joint capital and found that it amounted to one dollar and thirty cents. There was no possibility of getting any more anywhere.

Late on Christmas morning we walked down to a hotel—walked to save carfare—and had our dinner, after carefully estimating the cost from the bill of fare. I should like to have a transcript of our conversation over that dinner. We drew a picture of the United States covered with schools teaching Gregg Shorthand, we pledged each other's health, we stood up and shook hands over it, and vowed to continue with this thing in which we believed with all our hearts and souls until we had relieved the young people the world over from the drudgery of learning the old systems.

In figuring over the meal we had reserved ten cents for carfare home—we had not thought of any supper. But the waiter helped me on with my overcoat—and away went the ten cents. We trudged home through the snow, and then Rutherford, who had a wife and family in England, played 'Home, Sweet Home' and other cheerful airs on an old organ until we almost wept. Then we went to bed sufficiently sad. That was our first Christmas day, and I shall never forget it'.[16]

The first weeks of 1894 were exceedingly difficult for John in America and Humphrys in England: both were desperately short of cash. Humphrys was struggling to keep the *Lightliner* going with very little support from the other agents who were negligent about sending him the money received from subscribers and careless about supplying articles for the magazine. Spragg, who had undertaken to write most of the shorthand, was infuriatingly dilatory. John placed a high value on the magazine as a channel of communication and as a source of encouragement to all Gregg shorthand writers, and was anguished that he could not send any financial help to Humphrys. In the first week of the new year John wrote:

I have only 19 cents in the world, and R's entire capital amounts to 20 cents. We had only 4 Dollars on hand on Saturday, and divided it evenly. I shall have no dinner today, but it is all right. Business has sagged off dreadfully during the last week as everybody is holiday mad, and I don't suppose we'll do much this week.

When he learned that Humphrys was proposing to sell off his family heirlooms to keep the magazine in print, he absolutely forbade it.[17]

John and Rutherford struggled for survival through the first bitterly cold weeks of the year. The newspaper advertisements were the only publicity that could be afforded but they did attract some pupils prepared to study by correspondence. John had a box in the Boston post office to which he and Rutherford would go early in the morning, and if there was a cheque for $1.75 for a correspondence course, he would immediately cash it at the adjoining bank, then they would cross to the alley where Wyman's coffee house offered buttered cakes and coffee for breakfast. When the weather was at its worst and pupils were few, there was an occasion when John had to live for three days on a sample packet of shredded-wheat biscuits, which were then being introduced. Thereafter he developed a strong distaste for those items:

There was, however, heartening news from those teachers who had

51

experimented with Gregg shorthand. In the February edition of *The Lightliner* appeared a letter from Miss E. A. Tibbetts, the proprietor of the Salem Commercial School:

> After a careful investigation of your system I decided, with little hesitation, that it would be a decided improvement in my school over the old methods of shorthand. I am satisfied that it was the wisest move I could have made. Not only are students making much more rapid progress, but the satisfaction depicted on their faces is quite a relief after the old dreary days of Pitman's rules and vocabulary.

John was also able to give publicity to the testimonial of Rabbi S. Schindler:

> I testify with pleasure that in my opinion your system of shorthand enables a person to learn it in a very short time. It is so simple that one can teach it to others with success: it is so comprehensive that when out of practice a short review brings back all that has perhaps escaped the memory. I feel sure that your system in due time will become the ruling system in this country.

It was extremely unfortunate that this farsighted pioneer was unable to convince his colleagues on the Boston School Board that the system should be introduced to the schools under their supervision.

It was clear that a change of plan was required. John conferred with Rutherford and they decided that an attempt should be made to win business in New York. John believed he should undertake the campaign personally, but Rutherford was impatient to get there, and although he had the greatest reservations in the matter, John agreed to his going, with the provision that after an interval of time they would change places. In the middle of February Rutherford left with the lion's share of the very small amount of cash that John could borrow.[18]

Rutherford's move to New York brought no financial rewards: in fact John found himself obliged to support him in his considerable expenses there. Within a few weeks John reported to Humphrys; 'New York eats up every cent I get. R. has moved as I told you, but has not succeeded in booking a single pupil and each week I have to keep supplying him'. Shortly afterwards[19] John writes: 'Rutherford and I have had a serious row. You were right when you said I wasn't in a bed of roses to have to deal with him, and I wonder what the end will be'. John had suggested to Rutherford that he should keep in mind the possibility of a shorthand enthusiast with money who might help 'the cause' by subsidising a lecture tour. Rutherford, far from scrupulous in money matters, had advised John that he had found such a person. John was outraged to read that he proposed to borrow a young woman's savings and give in exchange a worthless promise to repay with 10% interest. Rutherford had added cynically: 'We must remember our security is not worth a tinker's curse, so she is really risking her money. I shall not be fool enough to tell her that, but of course shall speak in glowing terms of our prospects.'
John immediately replied:

> Your letter this morning rather astonishes me. I am glad to hear you have got Miss

Shanks so interested in the system, but I don't think your proposal, if I understand it rightly, is exactly honest. Even if she consented, I would decline to put my name to a bill which I can not see my way to settle when it reaches maturity. The money is hers, and we have no right to speculate with it however confident we may be about the result. I shall certainly not be party to anything of the kind. I draw the line at getting a poor girl's savings under false pretences.

Rutherford had concluded his improper proposal with words which gave John further reason for displeasure:

If I work up the New York business well for you and make arrangements about this lecturing in my own way, will you agree to give me half the profits of the New York branch for three years? If you will, I shall go in with a will.

John responded:

You agreed to work up the business well, and put in all you knew, and now you coolly say, 'IF you do it, will I do so and so'. Most emphatically, NO. You conclude with, 'This means business' which indicates that you think you could do it if you liked.

To Humphrys John wrote:

Altogether things are unsatisfactory, and I am rather gloomy over the business. Here I am in debt to the printer, greatly in arrears to the landlord,[20] and responsible for 70 Dollars or so of Rutherford's arrears as well, and I do not know what course R. may adopt at any moment. We are linked together like galley slaves. I got in 30 Dollars last week, but in New York the total receipts amounted to 2 Dollars and the expenses swallowed this up, not to speak of rent and R's living, etc. . . . . . As I have sent R. every cent I could spare, I have not been able to put in an advertisement for three weeks, and you can well imagine that business suffers in consequence.

In mid-April, when momentarily influenced by sickness, hunger and despair, John composed a letter to the great publishing firm of Charles Scribner and Sons, in which he gave an account of the success of the system in England and the prospects for it in America. He quoted Rabbi Schindler's testimonial and those of others, and referred to the difficulty of continuing business in both countries, and offered the American copyright for $250. He received no reply.

Business improved during the spring at Boston, but Rutherford continued to be a worry. He had not moved from New York and was soaking up the greater part of all that John earned. Humphrys learned on the 10th April:

Today I had a letter of four closely written sheets in shorthand from Rutherford which consisted of nothing but a pitiable recital of all his woes, real and imaginary, and it isn't comfortable reading. He is awfully changeable in his temper, one day he is right up in the sky, the next he is down to the uttermost depths. His letter this morning is one mass of contradictions: he appears to have changed his mind several times while writing it. He is going to take a position and teach in the evenings: he is coming back to Boston; he is going to stick to the New York place until he has got the money back; he is going to—oh, that is enough.

When John learned that Rutherford had a month's notice to leave the desk which he rented in a New York office, he wrote urging him to venture out to New England on a lecture and teaching campaign. To Humphrys he confided: 'If he remains in New York he will get deeper into the morass—the enthusiasm and the 'GO' is out of him. If he strikes a new place he will have excitement and vitality, and may meet with success. I hope he does'.

Unfortunately Rutherford would not take good advice. He wrote to John that he intended to return to Boston, and, apparently spoilt by John's subsidy, announced that he was repudiating their agreement to share in the expenses of the next printing of the textbooks, and moreover, demanded an interest in the copyright. John replied that he would insist on his paying his proportion until such time as their contract was revoked; but, even as he wrote he realised that the event was shortly to happen.

By June 1894 Rutherford had drifted into a commercial or teaching position, and John had begun the lecturing campaign which his former partner would not tackle. He visited the towns in a wide radius around Boston, concentrating his attention upon Worcester and Waltham, where he met with considerable success. Frequently Louis Pfeiffer went with him as an agreeable companion and unpaid assistant to aid him by picking up questions from the audience which John could not hear. Louis Pfeiffer also acted as a demonstrator, for he was by then very fluent in Gregg shorthand,[21] and it was particularly interesting to the audience when they heard how he had rapidly taught himself the system from the very same textbooks which were offered to them.

Pfeiffer was also with him during a second campaign in Rhode Island. On that occasion John concentrated his efforts on Providence, where he rented a small store which he furnished with little more than a blackboard and a platform and a quantity of textbooks. There John lectured repeatedly while Pfeiffer demonstrated that Gregg shorthand, with its connective vowels, was so flexible that it was possible for him to write from dictation, and read back, in any language, although he knew only English. He was very quick-witted, and a match for the aggressive enthusiasts for other shorthand systems, who, from time to time, tried to embarrass him and the inventor by demanding outlines for extremely difficult words.

A young man, Victor Frazee, who was in charge of the Commercial Department of Providence High School was among those who attended the lecture-demonstrations, and was deeply impressed by what he heard and witnessed. He purchased the textbooks and recommended their introduction to his own school, thus it became the first public school in the United States to adopt Gregg Shorthand. The results achieved at the school encouraged many other high schools to follow his example.[22]

Dr Pfeiffer noted how well they got on together, and, being a perceptive businessman as well as physician, he appreciated the potential of Gregg

54

Shorthand in America, and asked to purchase a share in the copyright of the system for his son. John courteously declined, explaining that his shorthand was so personal to him, and so closely associated with his life's interests that he could not part with it. Dr Pfeiffer then repeated his recommendation that he move to Chicago, where there was much more scope for the realisation of John's ambitions. When John was persuaded, but hesitated because of his insecure financial position, Dr Pfeiffer loaned him an amount sufficient to cover the cost of his travel, immediate expenses, and the re-printing of the quantity of textbooks required to support a major campaign. He further provided valuable references and introductions to personal friends at Chicago who would assist him in acquiring accommodation and business credit.

Louis Pfeiffer remained in Massachusetts where he made a successful career for himself in the wool business. He continued to teach Gregg Shorthand in nightschool for many years until family commitments impinged on his time. Although he and John Robert Gregg met infrequently in later life, they remained firm friends, and Louis Pfeiffer named his first two children Gregg.

At Chicago John was warmly welcomed by George Watson who was operating his small commercial school from his home. Watson was a well-meaning but timorous individual who was very much under the domination of his forceful wife. He had done little to propagate Gregg Shorthand beyond his own local area. John now proceeded to whip up interest by his usual methods of school visits and advertising. The response was gratifying, and as he had been told, the Chicago teachers and school administrators were much more willing to investigate the novelty than their New England counterparts. He gained a number of adoptions in both public and private schools and the sale of textbooks steadily rose, so that John felt confident about his future prospects in America.

But all was far from well in Britain. Humphrys was becoming increasingly burdened by the heavy administrative duties required of a single person devoting his evenings to looking after John's affairs. The agents in different geographical regions were squabbling amongst themselves; regularly ordering textbooks in advance of payment, and thereafter attempting to force higher discounts by withholding payment. Moreover, he was much embarrassed by the calls for the continuation of *The Lightliner* magazine which he could not afford to print. As more teachers and students took up Gregg Shorthand the quantity of administration and the expense of time and energy grew far beyond what one person could cope with; but, unfortunately the small profits did not permit paid help.

Whitford, although only authorised to act as agent for Liverpool, moved his operations to London and came into conflict with Miss Amy Johnson, who was doing well there and regarded his action as 'poaching on her territory'. She in turn allied herself with Tyndall for the purpose of publishing a Gregg Shorthand exercise book, without the permission or approval of the author of the system. At a distance of thousands of miles John could only apply to the overworked Humphrys to warn her off.

GEORGE WATSON   FRANK RUTHERFORD

A crisis point was reached early in 1895 when John learned that Miss
Johnson was about to give up her London school and agency to nurse a sister
who was seriously ill. John then knew that he would have to return to England
to deal with the situation personally. A London school and a reliable agent
there were essential, especially as the grasping Whitford was scheming to gain
control over John's shorthand interests in Britain. It was hard to leave America
when his salesmanship and energy were needed to continue the impetus of the
growing movement, but Humphrys was now ill, and the British organisation
was in danger of collapse. He left George Watson a large quantity of books and
literature, and arranged with him to take for himself a generous proportion of
the profits and deposit the rest in John's bank account at Chicago.

In Britain John dealt with the compounded business problems. He relieved
Humphrys of the duties which he had found unbearable; diplomatically
soothed the ruffled tempers of his agents; paid for a new printing of the
textbooks, and replied to mountains of correspondence from British and
foreign inquirers. For some months he so overworked that he almost
undermined his health, but he brought the British operations under control
once more. He then visisted his family in Glasgow before going on vacation to
the Scottish lochs.

By the end of August John was busy in London fitting out his office and
getting schoolrooms ready to receive the Autumn students, and once more he
had Spragg working with him. He remained in London until the end of
November, then, believing that it was safe for him to leave the British business
to the management of the local agents and the London office under the
supervision of Spragg, he returned to America.

CHAPTER NOTES

1. John Robert Gregg's system will be referred to as Gregg Shorthand from this point in the biography.

2. Rutherford had earlier taught a class of children at Boston.

3. On the third floor of the Equitable Building, opposite the post office.

4. On Harrison Avenue.

5. The possessive was used for some years; thereafter, Mr Gregg changed the title to *Gregg Shorthand,* being irritated by being called 'Mr Greggs'.

6. Published October 14, 1893 at Boston.

7. At 238 Great Road, Bedford.

8. According to an estimate made in 1892.

9. Invented by Jesse George Cross, 1835-1914.

10. *The Reporting Style, Part Two.*

11. Rabbi Solomon Schindler, Chairman of the Textbook Committee.

12. Wells Grammar School, Boston.

13. The Institute consisted of several small stores used as a refuge for newsboys and other youngsters from poor homes—with a separate room for girls. The intention was to provide educational and recreational activities which would keep them off the streets, and out of trouble. The discipline was reduced to the absolute minimum.

14. Miss Smith subsequently married Mr Lord, the Principal of the Salem Commercial School. The successful teaching of Gregg Shorthand materially contributed to the development of the school, which was in competition with other more prosperous institutions.

15. *Silver Jubilee of Gregg Shorthand*—convention report, p. 145.

16. He then added: 'But that dream has come true, those things we vowed to do have been done, and the work is going on'.

17. Humphrys' last issue of *The Lightliner* was February, 1894.

18. He pawned some personal possessions, and obtained a loan from Dr Pfeiffer.

19. March 27, 1894.

20. The kindly, elderly German allowed John extended credit. To repay him in some measure, John typed correspondence for him. Later the Pfeiffers provided him with an office in the Medical Institute.

21. He was also fluent in Graham Pitmanic shorthand.

22. In 1940, Victor Frazee wrote to Mr Gregg: 'Nothing I have ever studied was so fascinating as Gregg Shorthand, And no step I have ever taken did me more credit than selecting it for use in Providence High School. It was luck that it came along when I was diligently searching for an alternative to Pitman'.

Chapter Four Betrayal, Recovery, and Marriage

While in Britain Mr Gregg had kept in touch with Gregg Shorthand matters in America, as far as it was possible to do so by correspondence. Interest in the system was growing, largely by personal recommendation, among the teachers of commercial subjects, and more importantly for its immediate development, the proprietors of the private schools were inquiring about the advantages to be gained from introducing it to their classes. There was a need for a good representative to visit the schools and tell, in some detail, about the fine results achieved by those who had pioneered the teaching of Gregg Shorthand. In the absence of any paid representative, Mr Gregg had to deal with everything himself, and proposed to travel extensively as soon as he could collect the proceeds from the sale of textbooks which had been banked for him at Chicago by George Watson.[1]

On reaching Boston he stayed briefly with the Pfeiffer family, then he took the opportunity of calling on the few evening classes in Gregg Shorthand in the city and surrounding district. He left each group with an encouraging message, his assurance of interest in their welfare, and some words of his confidence in the development of the system. He then went to New York city to see Rutherford who had returned there to open a small commercial school. He acceded to Rutherford's request for the sole agency for New York, and allowed him a generous commission on textbook sales. While he had little confidence in Rutherford's consistency of effort or good business sense, he felt that because he now had his wife and children with him he was provided with a motive to behave with greater responsibility than before—and Mr Gregg left him hoping for the best.

He would have liked to travel much about the country in an effort to win converts to the system, but he was short of money, and limited himself to visiting school proprietors in Albany, N.Y., and Cleveland, Ohio. The Principal of the Cleveland Shorthand College, Alfred Day, was deeply impressed by Mr Gregg's advocacy for his system, and agreed to try it in competition with the Graham shorthand normally studied at his school. This was a major victory, for Mr Day had supported the Graham adaption of the Pitman system for over 30 years, and was himself the author of two well-known students' textbooks for the study of that shorthand.[2]

On the 12th December Mr Gregg reached Chicago and went to George Watson's home, eager to tell him of his plans for an extensive propaganda campaign throughout the Middle West. But Watson had terrible news for him. At the bank there was no money awaiting him from the sale of textbooks, because he, Watson, had embezzled it! He listened in horror to Watson's account of how he had used the money to open a branch school at West 63rd Street which he confidently believed would quickly bring sufficient profits to return to the bank the money he had 'borrowed'—but at the branch school those profits failed to materialise, and George Watson was unable to repay it.

After the first shock of realisation that he was once more without capital and obliged to struggle to propagate his system without funds, he took stock of the situation: it was pointless to consider reporting the matter to the police, and it was useless to recriminate with Watson. He knew that Watson had been acting under orders from his wife, who decided exactly what he should or should not do in his business, while he lived in terror of her violent temper and scathing tongue. Moreover he took pity on Watson who was being driven to despair by the fury of his wife on one side, and the financial troubles of his business on the other. Under the circumstances he accepted a proposal, made by Watson, that he should join their household,[3] where in free board and lodgings he would at least recover a portion of what he had lost.

Although his first few weeks in Chicago were exceedingly trying, he knew that his prospects were good: there was a growing interest in Gregg Shorthand and he had every reason to believe that the booming commercial and industrial enterprises would create a tremendous demand for shorthand writers. He had not the slightest doubt that Watson's branch school could be made profitable by better management and a higher quality of teaching. He threw his energy into the work with Watson's pupils and within weeks he had the satisfaction of receiving numerous enrolments through word-of-mouth recommendations.

On the 7th January, 1896, the Gregg writers of Chicago celebrated Mr Gregg's return to the city at a reception in his honour, held at Watson's branch school. At the conclusion of the function Mr Gregg urged those present to form an organisation for the purpose of extending the use of Gregg Shorthand and for the provision of pleasant social activities among people of common interests. He had in mind the shorthand associations which were so potent a force in European shorthand. To his delight the proposal was warmly approved, and within a week the Gregg Shorthand Association of Chicago was inaugurated with 40 members. In addition to the popular recreational activities, the association provided a pleasant opportunity for group practice, mutual encouragement, and the exchange of ideas, both informally and at the talks given by visiting speakers. The benefits to the members were considerable, and they led directly to the formation of Gregg Shorthand associations in New York and Boston a few months later.

When Watson's branch school was successful and educationally sound, Mr Gregg felt able to withdraw his support. Early in the Spring he obtained rooms at the Mason Building at 94 Washington Street where he established the 'Gregg Institiute'. Initially things were really difficult for him. In after years he remembered, with considerable humour, the occasions when he was obliged to barter shorthand lessons in exchange for dental services, for a much-needed bicycle, and for furniture. One of his early students, Thomas P. Scully, who displayed exceptional promise, was invited to assist with the school teaching, and John was then able to devote a greater portion of his time to 'missionary work' and promotional travel about Chicago. The conditions were right for expansion, and Mr Gregg could write to his new South African agent:[4] 'I have definitely decided to remain in Chicago, if Fate so ordains it, and to work from this great city. Chicago is undoubtedly the most progressive city in the country, if not the world, and it is a splendid place to work from in a movement of this kind.'

Mr Gregg considered that the greatest expansion of commercial education was likely to be in the public schools. He was therefore at pains to bring Gregg Shorthand to the attention of the teachers who were often reluctant to think about the introduction of shorthand studies for their pupils on account of their own memories of difficulties experienced in studying the older systems. However, there was increasing pressure upon the public schools to teach both shorthand and typewriting, a pressure which came from the pupils' parents, who were disinclined to pay for their children's tuition at private commercial schools. One of Mr Gregg's first actions, as soon as he could spare time from his school, was to write to a large number of public school teachers offering them lessons in Gregg Shorthand, free of charge.

As the number of schools in different parts of the country increased, the need for a magazine through which to communicate with Gregg writers became acute, and Mr Gregg determined to start *The Lightliner* once more,[5] although he knew from previous experience that it would almost certainly be sold at a loss, and that its production would involve him in a great deal of time which he could ill afford from his promotional activities.

The Lightliner appeared again in May 1896, with news of the progress of the system in America, Britain, Australia, New Zealand, and South Africa, and with pages of well-written shorthand for student practice in reading and copying. There were articles which catered for the teachers, and hints on the study of the textbook lessons specifically intended to aid those working their way through a course of instruction. As before, there were many quotations to encourage the ambitious, principally taken from Ruskin, Emerson, and Thomas Carlyle. Mr Gregg was able to comment with pride on the progress of the system during the interval since the last issue of *The Lightliner:* two years before there were only three schools in the United States teaching Gregg Shorthand, but in 1896 scores of public and private schools offered instruction. Gregg Shorthand was gaining recommendation and respect because the employers discovered that Gregg writers were more accurate and more proficient than those who used other systems, and the teachers were able to bring them to that standard with very much less effort.

A great deal of Mr Gregg's time was now taken up by his visits to teachers and school officials who had learned something of the success of Gregg Shorthand in other establishments but needed persuasion before they would venture upon a practical trial. Previously it had been necessary to argue from the fundamental merits of the system itself; now Mr Gregg could show the unsolicited testimonials of well-known educators such as Mr Alfred Day of Cleveland, who reported his best results ever achieved in shorthand since he adopted the system, and the letter of Edward E. Mielly[6] of Louisiana who had written:

Being familiar with all the leading systems of shorthand now extant, I feel in a

60

position to venture my opinion as to the superiority of Gregg's Shorthand over any other which has come under my observation. The Graham system was formerly taught in my institution, but it has now been retired to make way for Gregg's. I sincerely believe that it is only a question of time before Gregg's system will carry everything before it. I can not conceive how any one who knows anything of the older systems can fail to become a convert to Gregg's shorthand after a fair and impartial investigation. I consider it the greatest and most original achievement in the field of shorthand in 50 years, and believe that it is destined to revolutionise the art.

As more teachers turned to Gregg Shorthand the magazines of the rival shorthand systems grew virulent in their abuse of Mr Gregg and his system, but he, almost alone among the shorthand authors of the time, refused to behave in a like manner, and never commented in his magazine with more than a little gentle mockery at their outbursts. The publicity brought some humorous incidents too, such as the occasion when Mr J. G. Cross, the outspoken and self-opinionated inventor of Cross Eclectic Shorthand, called upon Mr Gregg with the intention of winning him over to his own system, and having failed to do so after long debate, marched to the door of his office, where he paused only long enough to declare: 'Young man, if you and I were united we could conquer the shorthand world'.

The gathering of material from abroad, and the writing of articles for *The Lightliner* absorbed a disproportionate amount of Mr Gregg's time. In the August, 1896, issue he had for the students an encouraging account of a self-taught young man in Australia[7] who had achieved a speed of 180 words per minute, and had been selected after a stiff practical examination as a reporter for the Supreme Court at Melbourne. Those who had completed their courses were stimulated to practise by such features as the penmanship competitions[8] which were run in the magazine with categories to suit writers at various levels of experience. The prizes, Waterman fountain pens, were modest in themselves, but the competitions urged many students to write with greater care than usual, which was very much to their advantage, and the schools obtained welcome publicity from the winners. It is interesting that in the second contest, in November 1896, two of the youthful prize winners were to be distinguished in later life: James Oppenheim,[9] then 15 years of age, was to achieve fame as a poet and novelist; and F. W. Colloton, then a junior stenographer, was to rise in the Church to become Canon Colloton of Toronto.

One serious problem was how to cope with the mail which had grown to mountainous proportions by the second year after Mr Gregg's return to Chicago. The correspondence relating to the ordinary school business was in itself considerable, but in addition there was a great deal of correction and written advice to be offered to those studying Gregg Shorthand through the correspondence course. As more schools and independent teachers adopted the system, increasingly complex documentation and accounting became necessary to record orders for the supply of textbooks. Although the sales progressed from month to month, the expenses of advertising and travel left small net profits which would have been swallowed if paid assistance had been employed, so he had to do the work himself—usually in the hours stolen from sleep. Over and beyond the regular business correspondence there was a steady stream of letters from enthusiasts who expected quick response, and not infrequently these came from intellectuals who had made shorthand their hobby. These persons, who might be expert writers of other systems, wrote scholarly comments and criticism of shorthand which often required several days' work to make adequate reply. Worst of all was the burden imposed by the foreign agents who were little aware of the difficulties under which Mr Gregg operated, and were in the habit of expressing their demands in petulant and querulous language, most particularly in the matter of deliveries of textbooks.

The most trying of all the agents was a Miss B. F. Tomkins of Dublin, Southern Ireland, who described herself as 'not yet 30', who followed Mr Gregg's recommendation to use shorthand for her correspondence, but who had unfortunately not troubled to master the system or write with correct proportion. She regularly inconvenienced Mr Gregg with twelve or sixteen pages of nearly indecipherable writing which formed the strangest mixture of business, gossip, and emotional explosion. What must he have thought when in one communication she interrupted her businesss report to announce that her life was about to end, and launched into elaborate instructions on the disposal of her valuables, and the accounts which she wanted him to settle on her behalf! Sometimes her language degenerated to an incoherence which suggests that her energy was fortified by quantities of the potent local beverage.

For a short time in 1897 Mr Gregg relied upon the assistance of a few of his senior pupils who volunteered to take and transcribe his dictation. That method was not really satisfactory because the students required a great deal of supervision; but the experiment was important because it led to an innovation in business education. Such practical work gave the students useful experience of what was required of them in the commercial offices they were shortly to join, and was recognised by them as a beneficial preparation. This 'work experience' was quickly introduced to the course of every student at the Gregg Institute.

It soon became clear that some of the work had to be delegated. At the end of 1897 he asked Thomas Scully to give up the greater part of his teaching, so that he could act as Secretary of the Gregg Institute, and in that capacity take care of the school administration. At the same time Mr Gregg set up a separate organisation, The Gregg Publishing Company, to deal with the programme of textbooks which he was planning. His experience had convinced him that it was necessary to provide Gregg writers with much more than a system manual, and he now had in progress a Phrase Book, a Shorthand Reader, and a Dictionary. One of the students who showed unusual promise, J. Alvin Shadinger,[10] joined him as his secretarial assistant and the first employee of The Gregg Publishing Company.

In April 1898 there were two events of significance: the publication of the entirely rewritten Gregg Shorthand textbook, which was issued in bound-book form—and thereby raised its status in the opinion of many who scorned the earlier pair of leaflets; and the first of the 'Gregg Shorthand Departments' to appear in the *Illustrated Phonographic World,* the popular shorthand magazine which catered for the interests of shorthand writers of many different systems.

The multitude of calls on Mr. Gregg's time and money had obliged him to cease producing *The Lightliner* after December 1896, and the void had only been partly filled by the importation of copies of *Tyndall's Monthly*.[11] However, the 'Gregg Shorthand Department' within the informative and well-edited *Illustrated Phonographic World* was to prove a boon to writers of the system, and it relieved Mr Gregg of one of his responsibilities because the Department was run by Walter Rasmussen, the Principal of the Shorthand Department of 'Wilson's Modern Business College', Seattle, Washington, a young man of great organisational ability, who was a recent convert to Gregg Shorthand.

Despite all his busy activities Mr Gregg had maintained his interest in journalism and his delight in collecting quotations, particularly those which gave encouragement to the ambitious. It was in the course of exchanging quotations with the lady journalist in charge of a Chicago newspaper column that he met Maida Wasson, whom he married in the summer of 1899 at Hannibal, Missouri.

CHAPTER NOTES

1. Whitford had not paid any of the instalments of the £250 which was due to Mr Gregg from the sale of the Liverpool school.

2. *Day's Complete Shorthand Manual 1889* and *Aid to Graham Shorthand 1887*.

3. The oldest of the Watson children was a boy; the next was a four-year-old girl; and the youngest, a girl of some months' age.

4. J R G to C. R. McKay, Spring 1896.

5. *The Lightliner* had ceased publication after the February 1894 issue, and did not appear until May, 1896.

6. The proprietor of Mielly's Practical Business College, New Orleans, Louisiana, was the first teacher of Graham shorthand to convert to Gregg Shorthand (in the summer of 1895).

7. Godfrey Simmons.

8. These competitions are characteristic of J R G's advanced ideas in relation to the study of shorthand. In the 1890s few teachers encouraged excellence in penmanship as an element in their shorthand programme.

9. James Oppenheim (1882-1932) chiefly known for his poems and his novels of *Dr Rast*.

10 He was to serve JRG faithfully for a number of years before leaving to establish himself in a successful industrial career. He was to become a senior executive of the Lockheed Aircraft Company, California.

11. A school magazine lithographed between November 1897 and January 1899.

Chapter Five Dangers Surmounted

The expansion of commerce and industry throughout the 1880s and the 1890s had a profound effect upon the prospects and activities of business educators and their students. Whereas, in the earlier 1880s most of those who sought instruction in shorthand were men who took up the subject as a hobby, by the later 1890s the vast majority of the students were adolescent girls intent on gaining positions in the offices of the merchants and manufacturers. In the earlier times the employers had resisted the entry of women and girls, but by the 1890s the women had proved themselves to the extent that most of the demand was for feminine office workers. By then the businessmen had more experience of shorthand and typewriting skills, and the standard of proficiency expected was very much higher. To meet these requirements the schools and instructors were obliged to improve their teaching. Because the public schools were slow to recognise the need for commercial education, the responsibility and the opportunity rested with the private schools.

By the late 1890s the commercial schools were sufficiently numerous to warrant their own professional associations. Two of considerable importance were the 'National Shorthand Teachers Association of America' and the 'National Commercial Teachers Federation'. Mr Gregg read controversial papers before each of them in 1899. Before the first association he criticised the prevailing method of requiring students to copy slowly and painstakingly the outlines of a shorthand textbook, and proposed the then novel and startling theory that from the very first lesson the student should be taught to write the outlines from dictation as quickly and freely as was consistent with accuracy. Before the second association he recommended not only early speed practice, but the use of phrases from the very beginning of study, and the early training of fluency in shorthand penmanship. At those meetings he established his reputation as a public speaker and was subsequently invited to address almost every major gathering of commercial teachers.

In the last years of the century the private commercial schools were increasingly under pressure from the employers to provide office workers trained to operate the typewriter by the 'touch-typing' method which brought such an improvement in speed and accuracy when compared with the older 'sight method'.[1]

By 1900 a moment of crisis had been reached, and at the teaching conventions of that year the school proprietors and the teachers exchanged anxious thoughts on what appeared to be an insoluble problem. Most of those who entered upon the commercial courses came equipped with only such education as they could obtain in the grade schools, and their parents could afford but a short period of tuition, seldom extending beyond three or four months. Almost the whole of that time was spent in intensive study of one of the varieties of Pitmanic shorthand so that there were scarcely any hours available

64

for typing instruction. The students were normally given but a slight acquaintance with the keyboard; thereafter it was supposed that they could gain speed and fluency in the day-to-day work of the business offices. When the employers insisted upon fluent touch-typing the schools were faced with a terrible dilemma: if they extended the courses to six or eight months to provide the necessary training they would lose the great majority of their students who could not pay for those extra months; if they did not provide the trained touch-typists, they would not be able to place their graduating students.

At the National Commercial Teachers convention of 1900 a number of school proprietors and teachers were able to assure incredulous colleagues that they had overcome the problem, and were successfully turning out competent touch-typist and shorthand writers in the regular three- or four-month session: they were teaching Gregg Shorthand, which, lacking the multitude of Pitmanic rules, complexities, and exceptions, could be taught in half the time and with a fraction of the effort required with the older systems. Several of the leading educationalists immediately sought out Mr Gregg and registered for his correspondence course, or like W. G. Brown, the proprietor of the famous chain of commercial schools in Illinois, made arrangements for a pilot study of the system at one of his schools.

The very successful results obtained by these progressive educators lent encouragement to the less daring among the profession, and a veritable 'snowball effect' was created by the recommendations of teachers and proprietors to their friends and acquaintances. By the summer, over 100 new schools were teaching the system, and the demand for competent Gregg Shorthand teachers far outstripped the supply.

The new century began well for Mr Gregg. There was a dramatic upturn in the sale of textbooks, and his school was thriving—then another disaster struck! On January 26, 1900 as he approached the Mason Building in Washington Street to take his evening class, he saw people rushing out crying 'Fire'! He learned that a fire had been discovered in an electrical showroom on the second floor. It did not appear to be serious, so he began climbing the stairs to his fourth floor school. He was met half-way there by a crowd of excited students, thus described by one of the Chicago newspapers:

> All were frightened badly, and fled precipitately to the stairway. Seeing the great danger and necessity for coolness, John Robert Gregg, Principal of the school, rushed to the landing and asked the fugitives to take their time. His warning was not heeded, however, and the scared pupils fairly tumbled down the crowded flights.

Raymond Kelley, the assistant teacher, then appeared and offered to assist Mr Gregg by taking to safety some of the valuable typewriters. But, as the firemen seemed to have the blaze under control, Mr Gregg said that they should return to the office and wait there for things to calm down. That was an unfortunate error: the fire spread beyond the power of the firemen to contain it, and by the time the two men, busy in the upper room, were aware of the noise and heat, the stairway was ablaze, and they were cut off from that means of escape.

They watched as a ladder was raised towards a girl trapped on the window-ledge adjoining their office. The ladder was just a little too short, and it was with great difficulty that the firemen persuaded the girl to hang by her arms until they could grasp her. By then the intense heat forced them to leave the room and stand upon the surface of the decorative entablature which ran the length of the building, just below the fourth floor windows. Through the swirling smoke Kelley saw a fireman at the top of a ladder beside the framework of a nearby advertising sign. He clambered down to the ladder although he suffered burns from the intensity of the heat.

It was impossible for Mr Gregg to follow. As the firemen could not reach him it seemed as though he was indeed doomed. But as he stood on the surface no wider than his shoulders he remembered his boyhood ambition to be a tight-rope walker and his long practice on the railroad tracks; it occurred to him that if he could keep his balance and walk along the length of the narrow surface, he could reach the safety of the abutting building at the end. He dared to risk the walk. Below, he could see the policemen pushing back the crowd, fully expecting him to fall at any moment. He concentrated, and his youthful experience served him well, and he reached the end. Opposite, on the same level, and separated only by the five-foot-wide service alley, was a window of the Title and Trust Company building. From his precarious position he jumped across, swayed momentarily, then grasped the mullion of the window and was saved.

A Chicago newspaper cutting, describing the dramatic escape, concluded with the words: 'Mr Gregg's loss is reported to be heavy, but it is hardly possible that it will seriously check his indomitable energy and determination as a teacher, author, and publisher'.

The next day when the crowds had left the scene and the building was roped-off to prevent access, Mr Gregg bribed the watchman to allow him to climb a ladder to the third floor, from where he could reach his office. He found that the only salvable items were some badly charred files and a quantity of damaged textbooks which were preserved by a steel cupboard over which the firemen's hoses had played. With such slight capital John Robert Gregg had once again to rebuild his fortune. Yet, it was in his nature that adversity only strengthened his will to succeed. That aspect of his character was described in a magazine article, written the previous year by Thomas Scully. When he had asked him what advice he could give a young man to insure success in life, he had received the answer: 'Perseverance, my boy, perseverance. If you lack that desirable quality, train yourself. If you fall down, get up, and never admit that you are beaten'.

Immediately after the fire Mr Gregg's business friends rallied round to support his recovery. Larger and more modern premises were found in the same street; the typewriter companies lent as many of their latest models as he required, and R. R. Donnelley and Company (then a small printing firm) set aside all work to produce a replacement edition of the textbook.

The publicity probably helped to swell the numbers of the Gregg writers. They had already become so numerous that Mr Gregg was unable to keep informed even of the more important people who used his system. It is remarkable that the most distinguished convert of that time, General Joseph B. Leake,[2] was a fellow-sufferer in the Mason Building fire, but he did not know of it until later.

In the same month as the fire, the *Typewriter and Phonographic World* printed an article about a most remarkable fifteen-year-old girl, Rhea Whitehead, who held a court reporting position at Scragway, Alaska, using Gregg Shorthand. Those proponents of other systems who were unfriendly to Gregg Shorthand rushed forward with contemptuous scorn at the idea that a girl of that age could achieve professional speed and fluency, and claimed that the article was an improper advertising stunt.[3] However, the scoffers were wrong: fifteen-year-old Rhea Whitehead was what the journalist had claimed, a practising court reporter, and one of the most brilliant early pioneers in that capacity.[4]

Mr Gregg's increasing involvement in the interests of the educational world, and the adminstrative burdens associated with his own business, obliged him to delegate more responsibility to others—but they had to be thoroughly reliable, for bitter experience had made him cautious. With deliberate care and patience he searched for, and found, a group of young, wonderfully talented assistants, almost all of them teachers, who combined a particular expertise with enthusiasm for propagating forward-looking ideas in commercial education. Some of them he met on his visits to commercial schools, but most came to his conventions; and, when initially, he could not afford to hire them, he marked them out for future employment.

The nucleus of early assistants included two young men of outstanding ability: Raymond P. Kelley and Walter Nenneman. Kelley had come to the Chicago school for practice in shorthand speed, and was afterwards encouraged to remain on account of his intellect and his intense enthusiasm for all aspects of Gregg Shorthand. Nenneman had been the junior assistant at the office where Maida Gregg worked, and he had regularly carried letters from her to Mr Gregg. His ambition was to obtain an administrative post of responsibility, and Mr Gregg provided the opportunity. He displayed a gift for handling figures, and was entrusted with the financial management of the Gregg Publishing Company—a post he was to hold and serve loyally for the rest of his life.

In order to combine a vacation with a family visit, Mr and Mrs Gregg sailed early in the summer of 1900 to Britain. There the low level of Gregg Shorthand activities was a source of disappointment to Mr Gregg. As he had feared, Spragg had failed to make a success of the Chancery Road school, and after some months of financial blundering, it had to be closed. Since that time most of the Gregg Shorthand teaching had been continued by correspondence, or through the intermittent efforts of Miss Tomkins at Dublin. In London they met Spragg and his family, and were pleasantly received by that irresponsible individual. Spragg wished to be involved in another teaching project, but Mr Gregg resisted his persuasion. From Spragg he learned of the recent history of Thomas Stratford Malone. Mr Gregg must have smiled knowingly to hear that

R. P. SoRELLE

RAYMOND P. KELLEY

JUDGE RHEA M. WHITEHEAD

PEARL A. POWER

the Script Phonography Company became insolvent, and was put into liquidation in April 1896—and that the shameless Malone had immediately started up yet another money-seeking company:

In Dublin they met Peter Murray, who, although no longer teaching Gregg Shorthand, assured them of his continued interest in the system, and expressed a hope that more Gregg publications might become available in his country. Mr Gregg also made the acquaintance of Miss Tomkins, and although nothing of their conversation has been recorded, it is clear that her eccentricity and waywardness ruled out any possibility of her being entrusted with a major campaign for Gregg Shorthand. However, the meeting may have stimulated her into producing the effusive magazine article in support of Gregg Shorthand which she published the following year.[5]

Their literary interests took them on a visit to Stratford-on-Avon, to Shakespeare's town, and there Mr Gregg, in his usual friendly manner, fell into conversation with a young accountant, S. G. Field. On learning that he was speaking to the inventor of Gregg Shorthand, Mr Field expressed an intellectual interest in the subject of shorthand, and Mr Gregg promised to post him a copy of the textbook—and then forgot about the matter because he was preparing for the journey back to the United States. He could not have foreseen that that chance acquaintance was to become his next British agent.

Mr G. W. Brown had been so pleased with the results of his investigation of Gregg Shorthand that he decided to have it taught exclusively in his seven Illinois schools. To enable his teachers to make the conversion smoothly, Mr Gregg laid on a special intensive training programme for the Brown schools at Galesburg during the last weeks of August, 1900. The Brown schools were among the most highly esteemed in America, and very soon other chains of schools, like the Massey and the 'Federated Canadian Schools', and a large number of individual schools, followed this example. The news of this revolution spread by letter and word of mouth with exceeding rapidity, and each month scores of schools converted to Gregg. The acceleration of this interest in his system astonished even Mr Gregg. By April, 1901 he could write: 'All through Illinois, Iowa, Nebraska, Missouri and Canada, Gregg Shorthand is now indisputably in the lead'.[6]

As knowledge of the advantages of offering Gregg Shorthand spread among the progressive private schools and the more enlightened officials of the public schools, so the demand for 'experienced Gregg teachers' increased. The agencies specialising in the placement of teachers—which were numerous in those days—deluged Mr Gregg with requests which he could not meet from his own school. It became clear that he would have to organise teacher-training courses at regular intervals. It was not sufficient to win converts from among the teachers of other systems, they had to be introduced to the methods of instruction and the ideals of practice which were specially suited to the system.

The summer schools, or 'Gregg Institutes' as they were at first described, were repeated annually in July at Mr Gregg's Chicago school for half a century.

As the numbers of Gregg writers and teachers increased Mr Gregg took two steps which were to be of importance in providing them with acquaintanceship and mutually supportive ideas. At the end of the December 1900 convention of the National Commercial Teachers Association, he formed the Gregg Shorthand Association of America from the 40 members of the Gregg Shorthand Associations of different cities who were in attendance. This was the only national teachers' association composed of writers of one system of shorthand. Immensely valuable as that organisation was, there was also a need to have a system magazine; so, Mr Gregg arranged to take over a struggling little publication called *The Gregg Writer* which had been issued at intervals since 1899 by Mr W. E. Van Wert of Plainfield, New Jersey. From January 1901 *The Gregg Writer* appeared under the editorship of Mr Gregg. It quickly established itself as an indispensable magazine for all who wrote Gregg Shorthand.

It is almost certain that Maida Gregg took some part in the editorial work of *The Gregg Writer,* though her name is not given as a contributor until 1906, when she took change of a new section, the 'Quotation Shop'. *The Gregg Writer* was intended to serve not only the student of shorthand and typewriting, but teachers and proprietors of schools also. There was a good deal of news of people and events mixed with practical exercises in shorthand and typewriting, and there were advertisements for business equipment. Among the educational innovations which were historically important, one of the first was a series of shorthand penmanship lessons. These were necessary at the time because few writers bothered to achieve consistency of size, proportion, or slant in their outlines, and most of the Pitman converts were so accustomed to the geometric angles of their former systems that they did not appreciate the real advantages which followed from cultivating a beautiful curvilinear style.

Mr Gregg was very willing to call upon the collective experience of the writers to develop the system. As early as November, 1900 he had offered money prizes in a competition for useful new phrases written in Gregg Shorthand, and when he took charge of the magazine, he arranged for a committee of independent teachers to judge the merits of the entries. The majority decision was that the best set of new phrases came from a twenty-year-old pupil-teacher at Bartlett Commercial College, Cincinnati, Pearl A. Power.

When Mr Gregg saw her contribution he was greatly impressed by her skill in construction, but he wondered more at the extraordinary beauty of her shorthand penmanship. The precision of her outlines in their proportion and uniform gracefulness exceeded anything that had been written before. He inquired of her prospects and ambitions, then offered her a position as an editorial assistant with the Gregg Publishing Company, and shorthand platewriter for the magazines and books. She accepted, and he thereby gained the services of an astonishingly versatile helper who was truly dedicated to the advancement of Gregg Shorthand.

Just before she moved to Chicago, to live with Mr and Mrs Gregg—as the first of several young people who lived consecutively in their household throughout the coming decades—Pearl Power's father volunteered to Mr Gregg some information 'which he would not get from her'. Since the death of her mother, a poet and journalist, when she was thirteen years of age, Pearl had acted as her father's housekeeper while at the same time pursuing a brilliant career at High School and business college. He and his daughter were quite alone in the world—without any relatives whatsoever. He warned Mr Gregg that her position with him would be temporary—she was possessed of such talent and determination that she was bound to make an independent career for herself at some time in the future.

Whatever expectations Mr Gregg had of Pearl Power, her performance soared high above them. Her flawless penmanship notes served as a model for students' imitation for years; she proved to be an able journalist; a tireless worker in the organisation of the Gregg Shorthand Association conventions and teacher training summer schools; and, as a personal assistant she cooperated with Mr Gregg in the heavy administration of his office in the busy first years of the century.

Mr Gregg and his assistants expended a great deal of energy in planning and writing a series of books which were to supplement the textbook. First, there was *Progressive Exercises in Gregg Shorthand* then a *Reading Book* to give practice in reading shorthand outlines, then, the first *Gregg Shorthand Dictionary,* and the *Phrase Book,* with outlines written by Pearl Power. Those were followed by the first of many pieces of literature rendered into shorthand: *Letters of a Self-made Merchant to his Son,* by George Horace Lorimer.

Many of the teachers from the schools which adopted the system offered helpful comments and constructive criticism. All of this was carefully considered, and where Mr Gregg felt it was advantageous, it was incorporated into the textbooks. In 1902 there was a completely new textbook, *Gregg Shorthand, Revised Edition.*[7] It was acclaimed as a beautifully simple but thoroughly comprehensive exposition of the system. It is historically interesting as being the last edition to have the shorthand outlines written by Mr Gregg.

Also in 1902, the Gregg Publishing Company issued a touch-typing manual which was for many years to be used side by side with the Gregg Shorthand textbook in thousands of commercial schools. This was *Rational Typewriting,* based on a manuscript having some ingenious ideas about the application of the four-fingers method by Ida Cutler, but entirely rewritten and put into practical textbook form by Rupert P. SoRelle, a very bright young man who came to the Gregg Publishing Company from the Armour Institute at Chicago. Subsequently in the course of his long association with Mr Gregg, Mr SoRelle was to write or edit a considerable list of educational books on Business English and Shorthand, intended for both teachers and pupils.

At the beginning of the century Mr Gregg became an American citizen. By then he had won the respect of the leading educationalists by his contributions to the profession, and honours and distinctions were extended to him. In 1901 he was elected to the executive of the National Shorthand Teachers Association, and in the following year he was invited to join the exclusive 'Willis-Byrom Club' whose twenty members represented the outstanding shorthand authors, scholars and historians of the world.[8]

Mr and Mrs Gregg's circle of friends and acquaintances widened to include many prominent Chicago literary and professional people. Among Mr Gregg's special friends was the eminent criminal lawyer, Clarence Seward Darrow.[9] Maida Gregg had introduced him to his wife, Ruby, and the pair were married from the Gregg home in the summer of 1903. Mr Darrow and Mr Gregg both frequented a gentlemen's club where, curiously, Mr Gregg's boyhood interests brought him into prominence. Several of the members were veterans of the Civil War who delighted in relating anecdotes about their adventures. When, as often happened, the name of a person or place or date escaped their memory, Mr Gregg supplied it. They were perfectly astonished that some one who was not born at the time, and came from another country, could have such knowledge. They were deeply impressed when he told them of his extensive reading on the subject while a law clerk in Scotland.

The expanding demand for secretarial workers encouraged progressive young teachers to set up business schools of their own. Most of these adopted Gregg Shorthand, both for its intrinsic qualities and for the reason that their experience had shown that its simplicity greatly reduced the large percentage of 'drop-outs' normally expected on Pitmanic courses. With good management most of the new schools prospered in the cities; but in the smaller towns there was often a conflict between the new Gregg schools and the older-established Pitman schools vying for a limited number of local students.

Mr Gregg was drawn as a mediator into a dispute at Trenton, New Jersey. Mr John Edward Gill (formerly a teacher of Gregg Shorthand at the highly-reputed Gem City Business College, Quincy, Illinois) moved to Trenton and purchased the Stewart School; at almost the same time the older Rider Business College[10] was acquired by Franklin Benjamin Moore, and a bitter rivalry grew up between them. Mr Gregg was acquainted with Mr Moore through their mutual membership of professional associations, and was grieved to think of the two proprietors dissipating the greater part of their energies and resources in a fierce struggle which was threatening the continued existence of both schools. He was able to bring them together and persuade them to amalgamate their schools. Mr Gill purchased an interest in the Rider-Moore School of Business and took charge of the Shorthand Department where Gregg Shorthand was introduced. Mr Gill was to train several young people who were to win distinction, and one of them, Charles Lee Swem, was to become the world's Shorthand Champion. The partners were gratified to witness the continuing prosperity of the college for the remaining 33 years of their lives.[11]

The textbook publishers and the vendors of correspondence courses in numerous varieties of Pitmanic shorthand were filled with dismay at the rapid and continuing conversion of teachers to Gregg Shorthand. They called a truce to their long-standing squabbles concerning which of their modifications was the most satisfactory 'improvement' upon the original Isaac Pitman system, and concentrated upon attacking Gregg Shorthand. Most of the Pitmanic system adaptions had their own journals, and furious denunciations of Gregg were made in the *Student's Journal* (Graham), the *Shorthand Writer* (Success), and the *Phonographic Magazine* (Ben Pitman). Such writing had little effect because their circulations were limited and declining as the tide turned towards Gregg.[12] Most of the Pitmanic publicity and advertising was done in the pages of the *Typewriter and Phonographic World* whose impartial approach to all systems of shorthand was able to hold the interest of those readers who had changed their shorthand allegiance.

As Gregg Shorthand had proved its qualities beyond doubt in respect to ease of teaching and learning, and equally in the matter of legibility and accuracy, those who feared and hated the system were reduced to making false assertions that high speed was scarcely possible because of the longer outlines with their inclusive vowels. In this they were using for their own purpose the old fallacy that brevity of outline is essential to obtain high speed; whereas the truth is that the principal requirement is quickness of mental decision with regard to the form of the outline to be written. In that respect Pitmanic writers were very much at a disadvantage because almost every word required a complex mental process to apply a difficult theory structure, and to analyse the sounds to produce a vowel-free skeleton of compact form.

Mr Gregg referred to the propaganda campaign in a letter to Mr E. J. Deason[13] of September, 1902: 'The question of speed has not cut much figure until recently; it is now the last ditch with our opponents. All their publications are taking up the cry "Speed".' When writing this he had in mind a particularly unscrupulous piece of propaganda which had appeared in the previous month's *Typewriter and Phonographic World* written by Fred Irland, the overbearing champion of the Graham writers. He had printed, in the 'Graham Department', a long reply to a 'request for information on the value of a joined-vowel lightline system' in which he had poured violent scorn upon Gregg Shorthand and its speed possibilities, and finally dismissed it as worthless. The intemperance of his language and the manner in which he perverted facts so outraged the readership that the editor was obliged to promise that there would be no repetition of such offensive material.

In the very next issue of the magazine, Mr Gregg countered the false allegations of restricted speed in his system by giving an account of the Gregg Shorthand Association convention at Peora, Illinois, in July, when Joseph A. Kucera (21 years of age the previous day) had demonstrated his ability to take dictation for five minutes at 200 words per minute, and followed that with a one-minute dictation at 225 w.p.m. While the latter dictation was in progress, Pearl Power took the same material with her notebook on her knee, and subsequently read back the text accurately.

Also in that issue was a call from the National Shorthand Teachers Association for properly conducted speed tests which could put an end to the inflated claims made by excessively enthusiastic but ill-informed supporters of the different systems, and the blatant dishonesty of some.[14] Unfortunately, the association's good intentions were nullified by the prejudice and malignity of some of the interested parties, and when after long delays the tests were held, the unscientific manner of the assessments provoked more argument than agreement.

For years Mr Irland and his fellow conspirators conducted a campaign of vicious disparagement of Gregg Shorthand. In part this was motivated by the arrogant bigotry of the man who believed that the Graham system was indisputably the finest in the world and that he was the best writer of that system, and in part by his obsessive desire for publicity in the shorthand world. Fred Irland was indeed a highly accomplished writer who had spent 25 years in court and Congressional reporting, but he was wholly unable to recognise merit in the writers of other systems, and his unscrupulous methods of achieving superiority led him to indulge in disgraceful behaviour.

At the National Shorthand Teachers Association convention at Cincinnati in December 1903, Irland arranged with some acquaintances an elaborate plan to embarrass Mr Gregg and his system. Unfortunately for them, it did not go quite according to plan, and the Washington and New York newspapers reported:

> How Mr Irland came to exhibit his skill and facility in writing shorthand is an interesting story. For some months he has been engaged in a controversy with Mr Gregg, author of a new system of shorthand in which he stoutly maintained the supremacy of the Pitman system. He was desirous of demonstrating the soundness of his assertions by an open exhibition at the meeting of the association, but as its rules forbade speed tests he was in a quandary. He had a blackboard made to his fancy, and this he shipped to Cincinnati, trusting to good fortune to help him.

The association members had wondered about a very large and solid blackboard which had appeared in the room where they were discussing teaching methods, and near the end of their session they discovered its purpose. For, although the programme was running late, the chairman, Mr Platt, declared: 'If any one desires to speak a few minutes on the original topic (style and speed in dictation) they have the privilege'. Whereupon Mr Temple from Washington, D.C., jumped up and offered information about the Congressional Record reports which he used with his students. Notwithstanding the fact that his professional card proclaimed: 'Blackboard demonstrations a speciality', he declined to use the blackboard, but called upon 'my friend, Mr Irland' to write for him. The special blackboard was brought forward, but Mr Irland protested 'God have mercy upon me. I don't know about this'.[15] He tried a few outlines, then said: 'This blackboard business is new to me, but I am surprised to find how easily it goes'. Mr Temple then produced a book of Congressional Reports, which he just happened to have with him, and proceeded to dictate to Mr Irland with great rapidity. After a minute there were 205 words on the board. Irland then started to read back. But, finding himself in difficulties at various points, had to be helped by Mr Temple. In the course of his reading back he made various blunders, which Pearl Power corrected. Irland was indignant and declared that she was wrong, and the dictator backed him up. The official convention reporter was asked to arbitrate, and he confirmed that Pearl Power's corrections were accurate.

Then the conspirators asked twenty-year-old Raymond Kelley to write on the board, because Mr Irland 'wanted to see what Congressional material looked like in Gregg Shorthand'. Kelley truly had no experience of blackboard speedwriting, nor Irland's daily practice in the vocabulary of political debate, but he took Mr Temple's dictation—in a passage of very much greater difficulty[16] than the first—at a speed of 160 w.p.m. After Kelley had read back correctly, Pearl Power (who was accustomed to blackboard writing) wished to take some dictation at Irland's speed. But the chairman rejected Mr Gregg's request that she should write, because 'there was not time'.

Immediately after these proceedings Irland released to the press a previously prepared report of how he had written 205 w.p.m. and he had triumphed over the Gregg Shorthand champion who could only write 160 w.p.m., and he accompanied it with a photograph of himself posing beside a blackboard displaying what was purported to be his Cincinnati writing. Fortunately Irland's deception was revealed to the shorthand world when Mr Gregg, noticing that the outlines were superior to those he remembered from the Cincinnati demonstration, examined the published photographs with a magnifying glass. He saw that there, in the corner of the special blackboard, was a clearly written date a month before the Cincinnati convention! Mr Irland who was so unused to blackboard writing, had been practising his material on it for weeks before.

Happily only a small proportion of the Pitman writers took a hostile attitude towards Gregg Shorthand. Many of the leading authorities on those systems expressed their interest in Gregg Shorthand, and even, at times spoke with envy of the flexibility of a system which could record so legibly the phonetic sounds of speech. The veteran Pitmanic reporter and scholar, David Woolf Brown, while in correspondence with Mr Gregg concerning the reprinting of his classic shorthand study *The Factors of Shorthand Speed,* had expressed himself in these words: 'I should be glad to penetrate, if I can, the secret of its success [Gregg Shorthand] which is phenomenal, judging from the enthusiasm of its practitioners and the number of schools into which it has been introduced'.

As early as 1901, the editor of the *Medical Visitor,* A. Smith, MD, who had learned Gregg Shorthand, commented that in his opinion 'it is peculiarly adapted to scientific work'. In the next year another convert, Camilo E. Pani, who wrote the Spanish Marti system, discovered how fluent were the forms of Spanish words written in Gregg Shorthand characters, and subsequently published his Spanish Gregg Shorthand textbook, which was the first of the great many adaptions to other languages. The full awareness of the ease with which the system could cope with foreign languages came in 1904, at the St. Louis Exposition, where Raymond Kelley demonstrated his ability to take dictation in twenty different languages from the foreign visitors, successfully reading back the phonetic symbols he had written.

The wonderfully rapid acceptance of Gregg Shorthand among the private and public schools of America and Canada aroused the malicious envy of some individuals who sought to enrich themselves by pirating and plagiarising the system. One of the first and most objectionable of these was Frederick Willis Mosher, who in character and career bore a considerable resemblance to Malone. Like Malone, Mosher had nothing original to offer the commercial world, but he was very pleased to steal other people's ideas and inventions, and he had a similar propensity to litigation when the cost was not to be met by himself. Having failed to make his fortune by means of a textbook called the *Practical Stenographer,* which he advertised as an 'improvement on Graham's shorthand', he tried selling typing charts which were taken from the unpublished ideas of a Mr John C. Lowe, one of the pioneers of touch-typing, who lived beside Mosher in the city of Omaha. He was particularly annoyed when the Gregg Publishing Company's *Rational Typewriting* swept away the cruder instruction methods, and in response he decided to plagiarise Mr Gregg's shorthand system. In this he was financially supported by the Rohrbough Brothers, who were harbouring ill-will towards Mr Gregg because he had not entered into a contract to allow them 'exclusive control of Gregg Shorthand publications in Nebraska'.

Mosher and his partners issued a textbook in which the Gregg system was adulterated by the addition of a few alleged 'improvements' which consisted of Graham system abbreviating devices in the form of vertical strokes, and hooks of various sizes and the omission of vowels. Not only were these difficult to write, but they destroyed the lineal flow of Gregg Shorthand. It was a senseless mixture which Mr Gregg appropriately described as 'an attempt to mix oil with water'.

The Rohrbough Brothers spent thousands of dollars in the production of an attractive textbook and conducted an expensive campaign in several states, but the gross inadequacy of 'Mosher Shorthand' defeated their purpose and scarcely any schools tried it, despite the persistent claims that it was 25% shorter in outline and therefore 25% quicker.

When space was purchased in the *Typewriter and Phonographic World* for a 'Mosher Shorthand Department', it brought little response other than distaste and incredulity from the Gregg writers. On the 9th October, 1902, Mr Gregg received a letter from Mr Wayne Canfield of Wilkes-Baree, Pa.:

> I have before me the October number of the *Typewriter and Phonographic World,* in which I notice a page of 'Mosher Notes' and also an Ad. of the 'Mosher (?) Shorthand'. What the D. . . . . does all this mean? I have gone over these 'Mosher Notes', and on my life, they are not much more than Gregg Shorthand pure and simple. I beg to call this Highway-Robbery—Plagiarism complete and of the highest order! Does your copyright not cover such thieves?

Mosher and his publishers circulated a news-sheet with the heading *Mosher Shorthand*[17] in which they taunted Mr Gregg and asked him to sue them—they were confident that they had devised a way of avoiding legal remedy. Mosher had taken all his Gregg Shorthand material from the editions which were published in England before Mr Gregg had come to America, and which were not protected by American copyright law, Mr Gregg replied to the taunts with advertisements in the Omaha newspapers which included the words: 'The man who is so small intellectually as to steal the work of another man's brain can never hope to see his piratical system attain much popularity. The knowledge that he is a thief subjects him to contempt of honest men everywhere'.

By January 1905, when only 5 classes in 'Mosher Shorthand' were left in America, the Rohrbough Brothers were bitterly regretting ever having got involved with Mosher, and were desperately trying to sell off their stock of unsold textbooks and their interest in 'Mosher Shorthand' to another publisher[18]—without success!

At about the time that Mr Gregg was thankfully free of Mosher, another troublesome individual appeared to serve as a thorn in his flesh. This was Lucius Clay Spencer[19] of New Orleans, the proprietor and salesman of a system of shorthand usually called 'Chartier Shorthand'.[20] He had purchased the rights to the system in 1905 from the inventor, Edwin M. Chartier who had 'borrowed' freely and without much wisdom from the popular systems of the time. Notwithstanding the fact that the crudities of the system violated every quality desirable in a modern system, Mr Spencer attempted to foist it upon the schools and the public through extravagant claims relating to the extraordinary speed with which it could be learned. A few school proprietors were induced to try it. That, in the opinion of a contemporary shorthand historian, James W. Beers, 'was a crowning piece of idiocy', for he believed that the Chartier system 'was the most illegible style of shorthand ever to get into the schools'.

Mr L. C. Spencer was determined to gain publicity through a competition with Gregg Shorthand, and persuaded 'The Spencer Schools'[21] of Jersey City, New Jersey, to challenge a Gregg teaching institute of the same city, the 'Drake School', to a $4,000 competition to be judged on the performance of students of the two systems.

Five prominent business men of Jersey City agreed to oversee the competition. The Schools obtained students by advertising for seventh- and eighth-grade public school pupils, and these were given six months instruction, beginning in April 1908—shorthand being their only subject. Tests were given to seven students selected by each school, at the end of four months, and again, finally, after six months. The assessment of the dictations[22] given was curiously unscientific, because only the correct words in each dictation were counted—making it a word-list test—no consideration was given to the quality of the transcript as a whole. Few teachers would regard such results as a good indication of the practical application of a shorthand system, but the committee of business men were apparently quite satisfied with that arrangement.

Within a few weeks Mr L. C. Spencer had organised a dishonest advertising stunt: he obtained (by means which were never revealed) a letter from the Employment Manager of the Underwood Typewriter Company, to the effect that seven of the Chartier shorthand students had passed 'his examination'. This was then advertised in the press under the banner headlines: 'Chartier students pass the regular test given by the Underwood Typewriter Company at the end of the second month'. Astonished commercial school teachers, knowing of Underwood's stiff five-minute test at 100 w.p.m., made inquiries. The embarrassed General Manager of the company, who almost certainly knew nothing of the affair, was then obliged to issue a corrective letter stating that the examination was not his company's regular 100 w.p.m. test, but a 'special test at the request of Mr L. C. Spencer, at which very easy business letters of one minute's duration were dictated'.

When the first of the two school tests was held, Drake School (teaching

Gregg) was found to lead by 246 points. L. C. Spencer was determined that his students should win the second test.

When the committee arrived at the Spencer School on the 24th October for the test which was to decide who was to receive the $4,000, the reader ('A lady from Brooklyn' as L. C. Spencer described her) objected to reading the matter brought by the committee, on account of it being 'too difficult', and insisted on selecting, from the school library, some material for the dictation. The committee agreed—when they did so they had no knowledge that she was a former teacher at the Spencer School.[23] It is more than probable that the Chartier students had been drilled on what the 'Lady from Brooklyn' dictated to them at the test,[24] and they dramatically improved on their performance, compared with the first test (they were 172 points in advance of the Gregg students); however, after the points gained in each test were added together, the extra points achieved by the Spencer students were not sufficient for them to win the contest. The committee declared that the Gregg students had won the stake money for the Drake School.

Even after loosing his $2,000 L. C. Spencer continued to proclaim in his own journal of tiny circulation, *Chartier Magazine*, and in the newspapers and commercial press, the most flagrant lies about the results of the Jersey City contest, such as the full-page advertisement in the *Typewriter and Phonographic World* of January 1909, where he called the reader's attention to 'Gregg's overwhelming defeat; Chartier's wonderful victory', and reprinted the misleading letter from the Employment Manager of the Underwood Typewriting Company. Before long people recognised his method of turning logic upside-down, and ignored what he wrote. Like Mosher, Spencer probably hoped that Mr Gregg would sue him at law, and that he would gain more from publicity than whatever he would lose at the courts—but he did not succeed. Soon Mr Spencer was left as the only person teaching Chartier—even his wife returned to teaching Gregg Shorthand!

The persistent calls for speed competitions from Mr Irland and a few others who wished to display their practised skill in the highly specialised area of court reporting, convinced Mr Gregg that he would have to train some of his own young people to compete in this line. In the earlier years of the century there was little opportunity for Gregg Shorthand writers to obtain the necessary experience in the manner which was normal to the Pitman writers. Most of those were trained by the older court reporters who, before the dictating machines became popular, read their shorthand notes to an amanuensis, who took dictation at a gradually increasing rate in his own shorthand notebook, and transcribed for his senior. The majority of the best qualified court reporters in the major cities worked for a small number of agencies who were at first considerably prejudiced against Gregg Shorthand—in all probability believing the oft-repeated nonsense about the 'limited speed capabilities' of the system.

One of Mr Gregg's first tasks was to gather examples of the specialised vocabulary of the court rooms, and convert the most frequently used words and phrases into suitable outlines. In this he was assisted by those Gregg writers who had experience of the court world—usually in the quieter country districts. From them he obtained many examples of their own devising, and these were added to compilations based on his work in the law office in Glasgow. In 1907 he issued the first expert-level book, *The Gregg Reporter.*

While Mr Gregg had complete confidence in the potential of Gregg Shorthand to match the speeds achieved by any other system, he was to suffer much frustration and delay before he could have the services of speedwriters of championship calibre. On various occasions he had working for the school and the publishing company writers who could at least equal, if not outstrip, the champions of other systems in ordinary literary matter, but those calling for speed competitions wanted to limit the dictation to the legal language of the court room, and although he did train several for that type of shorthand writing, Fate stole from him his finest writers just when he needed them.

Joseph A. Kucera was the first of his American speedwriters, but that young man's ambition took him into law in 1903. At intervals, a talented young man, George Niklaus, was with him, but he was unreliable, moody, and not amenable to discipline in the strict training. Both Pearl A. Power and Raymond P. Kelley were potential champions of the highest order, but neither was available, or in training, when their services were required. Pearl Power sadly had to leave Chicago in 1904 to return to Cincinnati where her elderly father was ill. Although she remained with him until his death two years later, she continued to run the 'Learner's Department' of the *Gregg Writer* and to produce her incomparable shorthand plates for the Gregg Writer, but she never again returned to championship speedwriting. Raymond Kelley took on more and more adminstrative work at the Gregg School in Chicago, so that his responsibilities there were too heavy to permit him to maintain his speed and fluency at the degree of proficiency demanded by contest conditions. The young man who took his place in training, Emil A. Trefzger, was equally fluent in typewriting, and when, in 1906, he distinguished himself in one of the amateur typing contests, he was enticed to accept a lucrative position with one of the major typewriting manufacturers.[25]

After some years of inconsequential discussion concerning the holding of an official shorthand writing competition, concrete arrangements were made at the Easter Commercial Teachers Association in 1905. Then it was agreed that at the following year's convention there would be two contests: one for writers who had had not more than ten years' experience, and another without any such restriction. Mr E. N. Miner, the editor of the *Typewriter and Phonographic World,* offered a gold medal as a prize in the first category, and Mr Charles Miller, who had purchased Rutherford's New York school, offered a silver cup for the second competition. Accordingly, the championship contests were held at Baltimore on April 14th, 1906.

Four writers competed for the Miner Medal, one being Emil Trefzger, who was then eighteen years of age; the other three were Pitman Shorthand writers. The winner was Sidney H. Godfrey, who had the fewest errors in the five-minute dictation from a current newspaper report, read at an average speed of 168 words per minute.

The competition for the silver cup,[26] for those with more than ten years experience, attracted four writers, including Fred Irland, the official reporter of the House of Representatives, Washington, DC. These dictations were also from current newspaper reports and the highest average speed was 203 w.p.m. All the contestants had great difficulty in transcribing their notes. After struggling for a time, Mr Irland announced that 'he was withdrawing from the contest', and later that evening he explained: 'That he was under the impression that the tests had been read at a very much higher rate of speed than 203 w.p.m., and as it was well-known that he could write much faster, he could not, in justice to himself, let it be known that if he happened to win the cup, he had not exceeded this rate of speed'.[27] The other three contestants failed to turn in transcripts within the permitted time. In truth, none of the writers were capable of taking and accurately transcribing the 'solid matter' dictated at the speed of 203 w.p.m.

The speed championship contests were repeated in the following years. In 1907 Mr Irland did manage to make a transcription in the Eagan Cup, but notwithstanding his loud and persistent boasts about his superlative abilities, he was humiliated into third place after making 69 errors in the five-minute dictation at 225 w.p.m. on easy legal matter. The first place was won by a Boston court reporter, Miss Nellie M. Wood.

After four competitions, the Speed Championship Committee of the Eastern Commercial Association decided that there would be a fifth and final competition for those with not more than ten years experience, and that whoever triumphed should keep the Miner Medal permanently. Mr Gregg was hopeful that that person might be a Gregg writer, and by this time there was a potential champion available.

In 1905 a young man from Zion city, who had been writing Gregg Shorthand for a year, sought the advice of Pearl Power in the matter of increasing his speed, and was clearly not dismayed by her recommendation to persist in intensive practice programme which he was already pursuing. This was Fred Gurtler, who developed into such a skilled writer that early in 1908 Mr Gregg subsidised his studies in the Chicago law courts. In the Fall of that year Mr Gregg hired him to inaugurate the Reporting Class at the Gregg School, where the course of instruction was to become the most illustrious of its kind in all America.

The fifth International Shorthand Speed Contest at Washington, DC in March 1910 brought victory for three young Gregg writers, and a complete vindication of Mr Gregg's confidence in his system and the certainty that its potential for speed and accuracy had been proved conclusively. Fred Gurtler was declared the winner, and two seventeen-year-old Gregg writers, Charles Lee Swem and Salome L. Tarr, took second and third places respectively.[28] All three set new records of performance on non-legal dictation, and Salome Tarr, who had begun the study of shorthand less than two years before, astonished everyone by making the most accurate transcription in any contest at any speed[29] (99.4%) up to that time.

These three young writers were, in large measure, products of Mr Gregg's

FRED H. GURTLER   SALOME LANNING TARR

policy of locating outstanding pupils and cultivating their development. Salome Tarr had been the brightest of the schoolchildren who had taken part in the Gregg/Chartier contest, and was subsequently invited to take up a post with the Gregg Publishing Company. Charles Swem had attended the evening classes at the Rider-Moore school at Trenton after a long day's work in one of the major industrial concerns of that town. He had so distinguished himself that he was recommended to Mr Gregg's attention, and he, too, was offered a place with the Gregg Publishing Company. Mr Gregg planned a programme of advanced shorthand study and speed practice for the young people, and this was supervised by Mr Rupert P. SoRelle during a period of several months before the Miner Medal contest.[30] Salome Tarr remained with the Gregg Publishing Company as an executive Secretary until she married a few years later; Charles Swem, who at the time of the contest had only eighteen months experience of Gregg Shorthand, continued his practice and was to become the World's Champion Shorthand Writer.

81

CHAPTER NOTES

1. Many people claimed to have originated 'touch typing' but there is no doubt that it was Bates Torrey who produced the first genuine textbook of the method: *Practical Typewriting by the All-Finger Method which leads to Operation by Touch.* (1889) The person who popularised the method was Frank McGurrin, who in the 1890s demonstrated its application to high-speed work.

2. Brigadier General Joseph B. Leake (1828-1913) the Civil War veteran who practised law at Chicago.

3. In all probability the Pitmanic journalists were sincere in their exclamations of disbelief. In 1896 the most eminent shorthand reporters contributed to a symposium upon the length of time required to obtain verbatim speed in shorthand. The average was 10 years! (*How Long?* Phonographic Institute Co., Cincinnati.)

4. Rhea Whitehead was later to use her shorthand skills to pay for her own legal education, and quickly rose to become one of the most distinguished judges in the American courts.

5. *National Teacher and Irish Educational Journal,* May 18, 1901.

6. *The Gregg Writer,* April 1901, p. 237

7. Mr Gregg's own copy is inscribed: 'First copy, to Maida, the memory of whose patience and forbearance while this book was being prepared, will ever be associated with it in the mind of Jack. July 1902.'

8. The club was formed by Charles Currier Beale, historian and reporter, in 1902, the 300th anniversary of the appearance of the first alphabetic shorthand system in the English language.

9. 1857-1938.

10. Founded by Andrew Jackson Rider in 1865 as the 'Trenton Business College'.

11. They both died within a few months of each other in 1934. The institution continued to develop, and as Rider College, moved in the 1960s to its present 333-acre campus at Lawrenceville, 3 miles form Trenton. Today Rider College offers undergraduate and graduate degrees in the schools of Liberal Arts & Science, Education, Business Administration, and Continuing Studies.

12. In contrast, the circulation of *The Gregg Writer* increased dramatically by 5,000 in the first months that it was taken over by John Robert Gregg, and it continued to grow by several thousand subscribers each month.

13. After a long interval Deason had contacted Mr Gregg and indicated that he was willing to promote Gregg Shorthand again in England, if it was made worth his while financially.

14. An extreme example of this type was the statement in *The Bulletin of Cross Eclectic,* September, 1906, which claimed: 'Miss Sinai, after 7 months study wrote 340 words per minute in shorthand'.

15. The official reporter for the convention was a Munson Pitmanic writer—but a separate report was made by Pearl A. Power.

16. Irland's passage had been carefully chosen, not only for its simplicity, but for its numerous repetitions of words and phrases regularly introduced into the daily Congressional debates. 'Mr' was repeated 12 times; 'Tennessee' 7 times; 'The gentleman from Ohio/Tennessee' was repeated 5 times. These were the expressions which Irland was writing as abbreviations during every hour of his professional work.

17. Decorated with the representation of a stubby hand between the words—a device copied from the cover design of Browne and Holland's *Shorthand News*.

18. W. L. Musick Publishing Company, St. Louis, Missouri. A firm which specialised in reading books prepared in different systems of shorthand.

19. Born 1866.

20. Known at different times by a large variety of names, including: 'Spencerian' and 'Spencerian-Chartier'.

21. The proprietor, A. L. Spencer, was not related to Mr L. C. Spencer.

22. Business letters read at 70, 100, and 120 w.p.m. in the first test, and 150 w.p.m. at the second test.

23. The facts were subsequently revealed by Edmond F. Mielly, the proprietor of a business school in New Orleans.

24. James W. Beers, an interested contemporary observer, made the implication when he wrote: 'There was apparently some reason to believe that the Chartier students had wonderful memories, but these memories seem to have been on vacation at the time of the examination'. *The Gregg-Chartier Contest* (privately printed booklet).

25. He rose to become the Vice-President of the Underwood Elliot T. Fisher Company.

26. Then called the Eagan Cup, because of a change of donor.

27. *Typewriter and Phonographic World,* May 1906, p. 342.

28. Congressional Record reports and sermons were read at a range of speeds. The contestants could choose which they wished to transcribe. The winner was the person who produced the most accurate transcription at the highest speed submitted to the judges. Gurtler and Swem offered the 180 w.p.m. dictation.

29. She submitted the 140 w.p.m. dictation.

30. Mr SoRelle published a description of the training in his book, *Expert Shorthand Speed Course* 1913, Gregg Publishing Company.

Chapter Six Persistence Rewarded

In the first decade of the 20th century the Gregg School at Chicago expanded greatly in size and range of courses offered. The school soon achieved a well-merited prestige both for the quality of its teaching and the efficiency of its graduates, for among all the institutions in the country offering Gregg Shorthand it set the standard to which others could aspire. Mr Gregg had recruited for the key teaching positions men and women of really outstanding ability as teachers, and in almost every case they were people bursting with ideas for educational progress and experiment. He encouraged them to express their ideas in contributions to the *Gregg Writer,* and supported the many texts in teaching practice, shorthand studies, English, and office skills which were produced for the Chicago students and subsequently issued as books by the Gregg Publishing Company.

From 1903 the Gregg School had the services of Frances Effinger-Raymond[1] who took charge of the Elementary Department where she was assisted by Kitty Dixon. Both were women of strong personality and admirably suited to providing their students with the basis of their secretarial skills. They believed implicitly in the efficacy of very hard work and the absolute mastery of fundamentals. Neither stinted on the efforts which they expended in training the students who left their classes charged with knowledge and enthusiasm.

Frances Effinger-Raymond applied her boundless energy to part-time court reporting, the writing of English texts,[2] and administrative duties. Later she was appointed manager of the Gregg office at San Francisco. Kitty Dixon progressively took over her duties in the Elementary Department and specialised in the training of thousands of teacher 'converts' both in the evening classes and the annual summer school, earning for herself the title of 'the best known shorthand teacher in the United States' before she left the school in late middle-age to marry a retired business man.

Mr Gregg was equally fortunate in the staff who served him as Advance Course teachers. In 1906 he obtained the services of Hubert A. Hagar from Indianapolis, a vigorous shorthand teacher and a fluent writer,[3] and an administrator of distinction. By 1911 he was promoted to become the manager of the Chicago office, and subsequently was Mr Gregg's right-hand man of business.

The Reporting Class flourished under Fred Gurtler and his dedicated assistant, Helen Evans, tempted away from her beloved Iowa by Mr Gregg, who had learned of her wonderfully effective high-pressure teaching methods during his attendance at professional conventions. When Mr Gurtler joined a partnership of court reporters working in the Chicago courts,[4] he had to reduce his teaching commitments, and Helen Evans gradually succeeded to control of the Reporting Classes which she extended to the day school. Her course was the first—and very many people maintained the belief it was the best—full-time training for aspiring court-reporters offered in America. From year to year the practical ability of Helen Evans-trained writers was her finest testimonial, and the best advertisement for the Reporting Course which attracted hundreds upon hundreds of ambitious Gregg writers who travelled from all the states of America to spend a year or two under the instruction of that unique teacher who was capable of qualifying beside the world's finest shorthand writers at the National Shorthand Reporters Association speedwriting competitions. A considerable proportion of those who attended her courses could not accept her domineering approach to the mastery of the technicalities of the profession, or could not bear the intensity of the work; but those who remained until they reached her approved level of accomplishment took their places in the courtrooms of the country as the best qualified and most highly respected of the profession.

By 1907 the volume of business in Gregg publications and the demand for service and information in the Eastern states was so great that Mr Gregg decided to open an office at New York. Accommodation was acquired in the fine Townsend building at the corner of Broadway and 25th Streets, and the Eastern Headquarters of Gregg Shorthand was in operation from December. He was assisted there by two highly dependable members of staff, Guy S. Fry, who was to attend to all the routine business on a day-to-day basis as Manager, and Rupert P. SoRelle, the invaluable editor, author, and shorthand trainer.[5] When assembling his staff Mr Gregg, characteristically, did not deny employment to a needy old friend: Rutherford, once again without a job, was engaged as a travelling salesman.

During the years in Chicago Mr Gregg had been so busy that there was little time left for social pleasures. Although he loved good company, his long hours and frequent travels gave him few opportunities to enjoy it, other than the evening gatherings at teaching conventions, or occasional visits to the Chicago Press Club. On moving to New York he determined to allow himself a little more recreation.

He became actively involved with the National Arts Club of New York, which was established in 1905 to promote the acquaintance of Art lovers and Art workers, and to maintain premises where exhibitions of the Fine and Applied Arts could be held. Although Mr Gregg was never a practising artist, he always enjoyed the company of those who were professional artists, and from the time when he could afford to do so, he patronised young people starting their careers. The National Arts Club provided him with much congenial company, and he in turn gave freely of his time, business experience, and financial support.

There was also the companionship of old friends with whom he spent a little more time when their business took them to New York. He particularly enjoyed entertaining two extrovert characters who made their own way in the world, and, like Mr Gregg, believed in self-help and enterprise. One of them was Elbert Hubbard,[6] the successful business man who founded the Roycroft Press, and is now best remembered by his series of 170 'Little Journeys' to visit the homes or work-places of famous men and women. Another close friend was A. N. Palmer,[7] the principal advocate of the free-flowing Muscular style of longhand writing which he introduced into thousands of American schools.

Maida Gregg also supported the Arts, but her primary interests were literary, and most of her acquaintances were authors or theatrical people. She presided over a regular Salon at her home, where she was pleased to entertain both established writers like O. Henry, the popular short story writer, and younger people who, she believed, had the potential for success. Mrs Gregg possessed natural dramatic gifts for which she had little outlet, although from time to time she did serve as a dramatic coach in amateur productions. One of her specialities was the training of actresses to scream realistically!

Although Mrs Gregg believed strongly in equal opportunities for women, she had no inclination to involve herself deeply in the business of the Gregg Publishing Company. Usually she appeared only at the annual Christmas parties as the President's wife; for, if she made any unscheduled visit, her commanding presence worried the junior staff, who were likely to receive her peremptory instructions. However, her manner with friends and relatives was very different, and those characteristics of firmness and determination which excited nervousness among juniors were a source of strength to Mr Gregg during the struggles of his first years in Chicago. He paid her a fine tribute in the *Gregg Writer* of January, 1902, when recording the marriage of a teacher of his own name, he wrote: 'May he have as much happiness in the blessed state of matrimony as this John Robert Gregg has done'.

In order to be free to attend the teachers' summer school, Mr and Mrs Gregg usually took their holidays in the winter months. On various occasions they spent time in Canada and South America, but Mr Gregg preferred sea cruising and from 1906, for a number of years, they paid visits to Cuba, an island for which they developed a considerable attachment, and where they purchased a small property. Even on holiday Mr Gregg could not keep aloof from shorthand discussion, and the writing of Gregg Shorthand (in the Spanish adaptation by Pani) was soon established on the island. At the time he could never have dreamed that Gregg Shorthand was to have a contributory part in the overthrow of the prevailing political regime.

During the years of successful development in America Mr Gregg had not forgotten his plans to establish the system firmly in England. He had been delighted when, after the chance meeting with the young accountant in Stratford-on-Avon, England, he had received an enthusiastic letter praising the system and offering assistance in its propagation. Some months later, Mr S. G. Field wrote that he had married and was then looking for ways to increase his income, and wondered if he could undertake agency work for Mr Gregg. The offer was accepted, and Mr Gregg recommended further study of the system, and promised coaching by correspondence. In the summer of 1901 formal arrangements were made, and quantities of textbooks shipped to Stratford-on-Avon, and much advice was sent to the new agent with regard to the use of advertising and other publicity used to win popularity for the system in the United States.

Unfortunately the circumstances in England were very dissimilar to those in America, and the chances of successful propagation of the system by a single individual working part-time were remote, no matter how great the enthusiasm and energy expended—as evidenced by the experience of Humphrys, Murray and Tomkins. Curiously Mr Gregg could not accept this: he had such confidence in the intrinsic merit of Gregg Shorthand that he believed that the Pitman system could be displaced by means of a moderate amount of publicity allied to a great deal of persistence and patience. No doubt that conviction had been strengthened by his American success, and his trans-Atlantic residence had dulled his memory of the strength of English conservatism.

From the perspective of time it can be clearly seen that, to have had a reasonable chance of winning a substantial proportion of the shorthand business in England what was necessary was a massive advertising campaign supported by a permanent English headquarters with full-time professional staff capable of dealing with all inquiries and correspondence-course work, and with facilities for teacher training. However, at the time Mr Gregg was determined to authorise only a low-level campaign at minimum expense.

For four years Mr Field struggled to build the business of his agency, working in the evenings, answering inquiries which resulted from his newspaper advertisements and the magazine reviews which he had been able to stimulate. He was rarely able to make much personal contact to encourage initial interest in his correspondents, and the proportion of textbook purchasers or fee-paying students was small. A little more than a year after he had begun the work he wrote to Mr Gregg analysing the difficulties which faced him, and called upon the experience of Mr Humphrys (who had confirmed that what was necessary was to spend £50 or £100 upon an intensive advertising campaign)[8] and requested that he be made a full-time employee. But Mr Gregg would not agree to the propositions. In all probability, his earlier distressful experiences in England had made him excessively cautious, although what was requested was well within his financial resources. There was certainly no ground for anxiety about Field's probity: he was as honest as Humphrys had been, and was extraordinarily conscientious, keeping meticulous neat and accurate accounts of every penny of income and expenditure. Although his faith in the system was staunch, he could not repress his bitter disappointment at the few pounds obtained each year, and wrote apologetically in comment of the figures—but he added the statement: 'I have not spared my leisure time in the interest of the system, nor grudged my efforts on its behalf'. He overworked and worried to such an extent that his health collapsed.

At the end of 1905 Mr Gregg learned that Field had suffered a nervous breakdown, and that his doctor had ordered complete rest for six months. For a short time his wife and a close friend attempted to maintain the agency, then they too had to abandon it.

In the summer of 1905 Mr Gregg received a well-written letter in shorthand from an English free-lance journalist, John A. Morris, a Pitman Shorthand writer of 24 years experience who had learned the system only six weeks earlier and was exceedingly enthusiastic. They remained in correspondence,

HELEN W. EVANS   S. G. FIELD

and when Mr Gregg travelled to England in the summer of 1907 he was
entertained by Mr Morris at his Liverpool home, where two of the Morris
children aged ten and eleven demonstrated their fluency in Gregg shorthand.
Mr Morris was very willing to put his journalistic skills at the service of Gregg
Shorthand, and had ideas about establishing another system magazine in
Britain, but Mr Gregg did not wish at that moment to commit himself to such a
venture. One of the reasons was that another potentially more important
business opportunity had presented itself.

Mr Guilbert Pitman, a nephew of the inventor, and for 20 years the manager
at Sir Isaac Pitman Limited, had investigated Gregg Shorthand to discover
what were the advantages it had over his own system which could account for
its enormous popularity in America. He found he could learn the system with
ease, and was amazed at the facility with which the outlines could be written.
Although he had twenty years association with his uncle's system, he became a
convert to Gregg Shorthand. He had by then detached himself from the Pitman
firm, and had founded an independent journal, *The Typist's Review,* and
appeared to have the capability and the willingness to boost Gregg Shorthand.
Mr Gregg visited him in August, 1907, and accepted the suggestion that he
should have the exclusive control of the sale of Gregg Shorthand publications
in England for a number of years.

As a convert Mr Guilbert Pitman provided exciting news for the shorthand
world and doubtless many of the geometric writers may have taken Gregg
Shorthand more seriously on learning of his choice; but, with regard to the
plans for the expansion of Gregg Shorthand in England, the appointment was a

disaster, and delayed the movement by several years. Mr Guilbert Pitman was not the person to give the system the vigorous and continuous advocacy which it required, and his ultra-conservative business approach was aloof from the enthusiasm of those who had recently taken up Gregg Shorthand and were looking for friendly advice, encouragement, and intellectual companionship. Very soon complaints from English writers began to flow to Mr Gregg's American office concerning the cool response given to their communications. Those who wished to keep in contact with the American situation were particularly hurt when they asked for samples of the American magazine, and instead of getting them received a curt prepared note which read: 'Mr Guilbert Pitman desires the writer to say that he does not stock the *Gregg Writer* but only accepts subscriptions at five shillings per annum'.

During his 1907 visit to England Mr Gregg had called upon Mr Field, and was pleased to find him restored to health and making a living as a Law Stationer and accountant. They remained on good terms for the rest of their lives.

Always exceedingly willing to assist those who had helped him in the days of his early struggles, Mr Gregg visited his Liverpool printer, William Blevin. Blevin had fallen upon hard times, and when in desperate need of money, had met Sam Gregg who had told him that his brother in America 'was doing well'. This encouraged him to write to America telling that his books still carried a debt in Mr Gregg's name which had been run up by an unauthorised printing order from one of his agents many years previously. He knew that Mr Gregg was not legally responsible for the debt, but he wondered if, in kindness, he would contribute something to assist him in his misfortune. Mr Gregg wired him a substantial portion of the sum and said he would settle the account when he came to England. Blevin was grateful and wrote: 'I have been so hard up this Christmas, that we have had no Christmas at all, or any expense whatsoever, being lucky in being able to go with the children to Mother's and a good Christmas dinner'.

Spragg had been in even more serious trouble: having committed some financial irregularity he had been clapped into prison. In 1906 he wrote to Mr Gregg mentioning his 'period of public and social disgrace, partly through my own fault (resulting from thoughtlessness) and partly owing to my having placed confidence in a certain individual who abused it'. He was then working in a menial clerical position in Liverpool, and wrote asking for 'advice'. Mr Gregg repeated the words he had used in a letter of 1901, unreceived by Spragg by reason of his being 'detained at Her Majesty's Pleasure':

I write to renew my assurances that if you come to Chicago, I will see you in a position within a week, then if you behave yourself, if you have gained stability with years, experience and increased responsibility, there need be no question about your future welfare. Away from old haunts and associates, and under these Western skies, a new and happier life would be open to you. For Auld Lang Syne I will do all I promised you, probably more; the rest depends on yourself. However, I am not sanguine as to your coming here. You will probably turn to your byways of speculation, if you have not done so before this letter reaches you. But you ask so seriously for advice, I give it to you.

He then recommended Spragg to organise a class in Gregg Shorthand, and sent him the latest texts. Spragg did not start the class; instead he wrote that he was unable to replace his children's worn-out boots and asked for 'discarded clothes'. Mr Gregg, realising that he was incorrigible, sent what Spragg described as 'a generous gift', and when in England, called upon him and left more good advice and further financial assistance.

Mr Gregg's generosity extended in ample measure to his family. Neither of his brothers had prospered, and he was able to assist them and their children materially. Before he left England in 1907 Mr Gregg arranged for Sam's nineteen-year-old son, Edmund, to emigrate to America. It was hoped that under his uncle's benevolent guidance he would be able to take advantage of the greater opportunities of the New World. Sadly, Edmund was severely handicapped by ill-health, and never could contribute anything to the Gregg Publishing Company which he joined. He was to spend many years in an office at the Gregg School at Chicago, where he isolated himself, surrounded by large quantities of dictionaries and encyclopedias, believing himself engaged in abstruse etymologic research. To the casual visitor Edmund displayed flashes of extraordinary brilliance of intellect, and could arouse wonder by his marvellous skill in chess, but his presence in America was a life-long anxiety to Mr Gregg.

In 1912 Jared Gregg's seventeen-year-old daughter, Georgina, went to live with Mr and Mrs Gregg in New York. She learned the system, quickly qualified as an expert teacher, then settled into the Gregg Publishing Company as a very hard-working and valuable assistant in the Shorthand Department of the *Gregg Writer*. Her penmanship was outstandingly fluent, and when the principal plate-writer, Alice L. Rinne, married Hubert A. Hagar, Georgina Gregg took on the greater share of the shorthand writing for the plates which appeared in the *Gregg Writer* and the textbooks. She continued to do this work after her marriage in 1919, despite the fact that she and her British husband[9] settled in Peru.

* * *

In the years before the first World War the demand for competent shorthand writers and typists increased enormously. The calls for such people came not only from business and industry, but government deparments also. In the year 1909, for instance, the Civil Service examiners approved 46,000 applicants for the 'Stenographer and Typist' qualification. The Gregg Shorthand-teaching schools were prominent in supplying this training because the public schools were being won over at a remarkable rate. In 1900, Gregg Shorthand was taught in the public schools of only 28 cities; twelve years later the system was taught in the public schools of 533 cities!

The principal resistance to Gregg Shorthand came from the very large cities

Charles Lee Swem reports a speech delivered by President Woodrow Wilson

where a complex educational administration obstructed change of any kind. In those circumstances it was necessary to convince individual shorthand teachers, then the superintendents, then the local government officials, and finally the city education committees: a slow and wearisome sequence of effort which ultimately brought the benefit of Gregg Shorthand to every great city of the country. From time to time Mr Gregg personally took charge of the 'fighting campaign', as in the case of Buffalo, where the system was exclusively adopted, after three years of trials, in 1910. A struggle for adoption also took place in New York City from the time of the setting up of the Eastern office in 1907[10] until the official acceptance of Gregg Shorthand in 1914. The Pacific Coast cities were among the last to be won. Mrs Effinger-Raymond established a Pacific Coast office at San Francisco in 1912 and conducted a vigorous campaign to bring the qualities of the system to the attention of teachers and education officials in her extensive region. She was a woman of large dimensions, imposing manner, and indomitable perseverance, and thoroughly skilled in every branch of shorthand from elementary instruction to court reporting. Within a few years she won another huge geographical block of the country for Gregg Shorthand.

The expansion of the system infuriated a few bigots among the writers of geometric shorthand, and they persistently attacked Gregg in their journals. They concentrated their attentions upon the absence of Gregg Shorthand writers among the top prize-winners of the professional contest of the National Shorthand Reporters Association. Their attempt to belittle the system by that argument was absurd: all shorthand educationalists knew very well that the quality of a system is measured by the performance of the great majority of the writers, not the feats of individual champions. However, the persistence of the critics irritated Mr Gregg and he determined to make a bid for the supreme prize at the National Shorthand Reporters Association competition.

In August 1911, eighteen-year-old Charles Swem astonished his more mature rivals when he achieved the third place at the professional contest.[11] On learning of Swem's performance, Mr Gregg commented: 'One moment after the announcement of the results of the shorthand speed contest it was realised by every one present that the last argument was swept away—swept away for ever.'

Charles Swem now set his heart upon winning the World's Championship, the first place in the NSRA competition, and would in all probability have soon achieved that ambition but for a series of events which were to change the course of his life.

Governor Woodrow Wilson came to address the people of Trenton, New Jersey, and needed a shorthand writer to report his political speech. Enquiries were made at the Rider Moore School, where Mr Gill immediately thought of Charles Swem, and telephoned to Mr Gregg to ask for his services. Mr Gregg, who had been a warm supporter of the Democrats since hearing the famous oration on 'The Cross of Gold' years before, sent Charles Swem to take the record. Governor Wilson—a fluent shorthand writer himself—was not pleased when he saw that the shorthand writer was a youth of nineteen; but, when the transcript reached him the next morning, he declared that it was the first time in his life that he had been reported with *absolute accuracy*. When he was nominated for the Presidency he requested that Charles Swem undertake the reporting of his campaign; and when he was elected President of the United States, he appointed Swem as his personal shorthand writer.[12]

However, Charles Swem had not forgotten his ambition—and Mr Gregg's— they came to an understanding that when President Wilson no longer required his services he would return to his training for the speedwriting contest.

Although Mr Gregg's writer had not won the professional shorthand championship there were other honours to bring attention to the system. One such was the award of the very first certificate of competence to report in the New York courts, made to Paula Werning—the qualification known as 'Certified Shorthand Reporter'. She obtained this after submitting to a gruelling examination in February, 1913, held under the provisions of the new state law for the licensing of official court reporters. The chairman of the Board of Regents was so impressed by Paula Werning's ability that he paid her a splendid tribute in his report on the first candidate for this professional qualification.[13]

Although Mr Gregg was always strenuously at work supervising the growing list of textbooks and editing the *Gregg Writer* and planning yet another campaign to win the trust of some hesitating educational authority, he somehow found the time to attend the teacher's summer training school in June and July, and the Gregg Association convention which followed it. Teaching was what he most enjoyed, for he was by nature and inclination a person who delighted in passing on information which he had acquired by experience. Something of his personal philosophy in this matter is expressed in the reply which he made to the editor of the *Typewriter and Phonographic World,* who had written in 1909 to four shorthand authors[14] requesting them to write a few paragraphs on the subject: 'Why I have devoted the best part of my life to shorthand':

Dear Mr Miner:
You ask me why I devoted the best part of my life to the propagation of shorthand. It was simply because, from the time I was ten years of age, shorthand systems were to me what puzzle pictures are to many boys today. I played with them, and worked at them, until shorthand, in one form or another, became an obsession.
As a boy I loved shorthand for its own sake—for the pleasure I obtained from the study and practice of it; but as I grew older, I became impressed with the conviction that, in a simplified and more scientific form, it could be made much more valuable to the world. This belief impelled me to make the advancement of shorthand a life work.
That, briefly, is the answer to your question. Shorthand got me very early in life, it has had me ever since, and it will have my thoughts and efforts to the end.
Cordially yours,
John R. Gregg

All who studied or worked with Mr Gregg agreed that he was a highly effective teacher, who had the gift of being able to transmit information in the simplest manner. Unfortunately, although he was frequently asked to write a comprehensive manual of Gregg Shorthand teaching methods, he never did so.

Because the demand for shorthand teachers was so great, many who taught other commercial subjects such as book-keeping, business arithmetic, and penmanship, were keen to acquire the skill and professional qualification during their summer vacation. Mr Gregg was insistent that they should have the finest possible instruction during the five or six weeks at their disposal, and neither he nor the staff at the Gregg School stinted on the highly-pressurised course. The vast majority of those who attended the summer school did pass the qualifying examination and carried to all parts of America a knowledge of the high standards which were expected—a measure and an ideal to aim at with their own students.

The Gregg School also operated a placement bureau for teachers which served to arrange exchanges of location for those who wished it, and to provide competent instructors to institutions looking for shorthand teachers. The reputation of that bureau was so high that the school superintendents and proprietors felt absolute confidence in any recommendation which it made.

As more and more teachers gave instruction in Gregg Shorthand the number of students requiring textbooks and magazines swelled enormously. *The Gregg Writer's* circulation expanded far beyond that recorded in any shorthand journal: in 1906 the circulation was 10,500; in 1912 it was 50,000, and that figure was almost doubled before the circulation finally stabilised in the 1930s. One effect of the system's supremacy in the commercial education world was that business fell away from other shorthand magazines. In 1912-13 five magazines closed, and in 1919 the famous Ben Pitman journal, the *Phonographic Magazine* ceased production. Probably the only casualty for which Mr Gregg had regrets was the *Typewriter and Phonographic World* which became unprofitable in 1912 and was sold to the publishers of the *Stenographer.* For many years Mr Gregg had tried to assist the sagging circulation by offering joint subscriptions, to Mr Miner's magazine as well as his own, at reduced prices, but the interest in comparative studies of different systems which had maintained the *Typewriter and Phonographic World* since 1885 had evaporated: the vast majority of seekers after quality in shorthand had found satisfaction in Gregg Shorthand.

The success which Mr Gregg was having with his system and his business excited the interest and wonder of rival educational publishers. In that connection an amusing incident occured in 1912, when he was attending a function arranged by the United States Chamber of Commerce. He found himself sitting next to Charles Scribner, the president of the great publishing house bearing his name, who engaged Mr Gregg in conversation, then confided to him: 'You know, Mr Gregg, we publishers keep ourselves pretty well informed about the trade of our competitors, and I happen to know that the Gregg Publishing Company sold more books last year than any of the rest of us. Tell me, Mr Gregg, what is the secret of your remarkable success?' To that Mr Gregg replied 'I owe it all to you!' Mr Scribner stared at him, and inquired: 'What has it got to do with me?' Whereupon Mr Gregg explained: 'Eighteen years ago, when I was desperately short of money, I wrote to you offering to sell the copyright of Gregg Shorthand, but I never received any reply; so I took that as an indication that the future of Gregg Shorthand was to be in my own power, and I persevered in my efforts to sell it to the American people'.

Mr Gregg did not restrict his company to the leaders of industry and commerce, for he was happy to know any one who shared his own interests. When, in the summer of 1912, William Smart, an English shorthand writer, who had been the secretary to Lloyd George, the British statesman, came to New York to take part in the NSRA speed competitions, he was surprised at his humble apartment by Mr Gregg. The person, who he had been led to believe was the hateful enemy of all Pitman writers, benevolently explained that he thought Mr Smart might be feeling lonely on his first Sunday in America, and had come with Maida's electric car to show him around New York, and to take him home to lunch. From that moment began a friendship which lasted until the end of William Smart's life in 1947.[15]

* * *

The sluggish state of Gregg Shorthand in Britain continued to cause anxiety. Mr Gregg made brief visits to the country in 1911 and the following year; then in 1913, he put into effect a plan for vigorous action. He established a school in Liverpool under the control of J. J. Jakeman's son Joseph; prepared an English edition of the textbook and printed suitable informative literature; started a new English journal, the *Gregg Shorthand Magazine,* under the editorship of John A. Morris, and set in motion a campaign. Mr Gregg had every confidence that this effort, properly financed and personally supervised, would generate continuous development. Even without any real organisation, the few English Gregg Shorthand teachers and their students had done very well, and reported their successes with pride to Mr Gregg. In 1910 and 1911 schoolboys took the principal honours in the College of Preceptors examinations, and in 1912 Ernest Crocket had won the Junior Shorthand Championship at the National Business Exhibition in London. The time seemed ripe for pushing forward Gregg Shorthand in the Old Country.

By a peculiar coincidence, Malone appeared on the scene once more. In 1913 another of his companies had been liquidated as bankrupt, and as quickly as ever he had registered another, the Script Shorthand Company Limited, and had proceeded to lure shareholders who would never recover their money. Malone usually approached practising teachers with his schemes, and in an attempt to win their interest he produced a substantial booklet which was an assemblage of the incorrect and dishonest statements of the past concerning the authorship of Script Phonography. It can scarcely have had much effect, for few people would have had the patience to persist in reading 99 closely printed pages of his wearisome rambling. Very sensibly Mr Gregg ignored it.

Before he left England Mr Gregg called upon Bernard De Bear, the one-time Pitman Shorthand champion, who was then the Principal of a chain of 33 business schools owned by the Remington Typewriter Company. With consummate salesmanship, Mr Gregg persuaded him to investigate the merit of Gregg Shorthand. He agreed to allow his daughter[16] to study the system.

* * *

Mr Gregg returned to America to take part in a joyous occasion, the Silver Jubilee convention of Gregg Shorthand at Chicago, held August 11th to 15th, 1913. It was during this convention that Mr Gregg reminisced about his early experiences and gave, for the first time, an account of the invention of Gregg Shorthand and the early history of the system and of his struggles to establish it in America. The crowning event of the convention was the banquet attended by hundreds of teachers, students, school proprietors and educational officials, at which Mr and Mrs Gregg were the guests of honour. Fred Gurtler, then President of the Chicago Law Reporters Association, presented Mr Gregg with a testimonial written by Elbert Hubbard and signed by thousands of Gregg writers. The school proprietors—who had prospered significantly by their adoption of Gregg Shorthand—presented Mr Gregg with a unique silver cup, 18 inches in height, designed and made for the occasion which was inscribed with their names. Mr Gregg, in turn, gifted to each person present a reproduction of the original *Lightline Phonography* textbook of 1888, issued like it in a limited edition of 500 copies.

A momentous boost was given to Gregg Shorthand in July 1914, when the New York Board of Education approved the experiment of introducing Gregg

Shorthand into the classes of the New York Evening High School and Brooklyn Evening High School. The city had long been a stronghold of the Isaac Pitman system, where conservative officials of inflexible opinion and those with vested interests in the maintenance of the Pitman Shorthand monopoly held out as long as possible against the demands of the teachers for a simpler system. At the same time, it was made known that Gregg Shorthand had been admitted to two of the largest universities, Columbia University, New York, and the University of California, at Berkeley.

There was now a tremendous demand for instruction in Gregg Shorthand by the commercial teachers of New York city. Several classes were organised, and the most experienced of the Gregg staff provided the tuition free of charge. Mr Gregg took part in the Saturday classes and attended numerous meetings at which he demonstrated at the blackboard and explained the most essential characteristics of the system. By February 1915 day classes had begun at the New York High School of Commerce, an institution which was to win prestige through the skills of its Gregg Shorthand-writing pupils.

The Panama-Pacific International Exposition of 1915 at San Francisco also provided Gregg Shorthand with a great deal of favourable publicity, for one of the pavilions contained the 'Standard Commercial School' where a regular business school was daily in session under the spirited direction of Clyde Blanchard, and the public could watch and listen to the lessons from a balcony surrounding the classroom. There were also frequent demonstrations of shorthand and typing skills based upon Gregg Shorthand textbooks which received the highest possible distinction by gaining the Gold Medal 'Award of Honour'.

A revision of the shorthand textbook appeared in 1916. Its principal characteristic was that a considerable number of new shortcuts for suffixes and prefixes were introduced, and many abbreviations which were previously used only by reporters were presented to the learner. The demands for these changes had come from the teachers who were accustomed to brevity of form, such as that used in the Graham Pitmanic system, and those who harboured a continuing anxiety about the visually long outlines in Gregg Shorthand. Their worries were groundless, but Mr Gregg gratified their wishes, and afterwards regretted it. Each following edition of the Gregg Shorthand textbook was to remove more and more of the unnecessary abbreviations of the 1916 textbook.

The outbreak of the first World War in Europe in 1914 brought new and serious responsibilities to America long before she declared war in 1917. At that time there was a vast increase in the number of young women and girls who undertook secretarial studies, particularly when the men entered upon military duties. The Gregg Publishing Company stepped up production to keep pace with the requirements both in America and Europe, and various special short-course textbooks and teacher's handbooks were prepared for the Army Education Commission. Mr Gregg became involved in a good deal of voluntary work, but his most interesting activity was one of counter-espionage!

The government Intelligence Department M.I.8 discovered that German spies were active within the country and were exchanging information in the

96

form of handwritten code. They suspected that it was connected with shorthand, and consulted Mr Gregg. He analysed it and identified elements of the German Gabelsberger shorthand system, and thereafter he cooperated with the United States military intelligence in the decoding of messages which the government agents intercepted. At the end of hostilities, he was warmly thanked by the Director of Military Intelligence for the valuable aid which he had given through his extensive shorthand library and his own voluntary services.

The experiment of introducing Gregg Shorthand into the New York Schools had been a resounding success. Each year the High School of Commerce shorthand writers, trained by Walter H. Mechler, won the lion's share of the prizes in the Metropolitan Schools Shorthand Contest. Of the 4,000 students at the High School of Commerce, the brightest boy of all was a certain William Rosenberg, who was some years later to be renowned as Billy Rose, the impresario, song-writer, wit, and financial wizard. By 1916 he had already won the title 'Shorthand School Champion of Manhattan', and in 1918 was presented with the silver medal awarded to the 'Amateur Champion Shorthand Writer of the City of New York'. The High School of Commerce students in that year won the first fourteen places in the Metropolitan Shorthand Contest, raising the average speed and accuracy to an unprecedented level for schoolchildren. The Pitman Shorthand-writing students were left bewildered and dismayed by their Gregg rivals who were capable of achieving an average speed of 160 words per minute after two years of instruction.

When the NSRA professional championship contests were resumed after some years of suspension, Mr Gregg returned to the idea of encouraging his young writers to try for the high honours. He provided coaching for Billy Rose and his prize-winning class-mate, Albert Schneider, and such necessary facilities as material-selection and expertly timed dictation, which championship contest preparation required. Billy Rose was very much the superior performer, and in practice returned transcripts of such unparalleled accuracy that when Mr Gregg left for a summer visit to Britain he felt confident that he would return to greet Billy Rose as the first Gregg Shorthand Champion of the English-Speaking World.

* * *

The first World War had almost completely undermined the organisation which was to propagate Gregg Shorthand in England. Both Mr Joseph Jakeman and Mr John Morris had been engaged in war work, so that few students were instructed and no teachers were trained. the only important continuing activity was the *Gregg Shorthand Magazine* which Mr Morris had valiantly struggled to maintain under very difficult conditions. Mr De Bear remained nervous and indecisive about the conversion to Gregg Shorthand, notwithstanding that he had had further evidence from a trial within his own schools.

Mr Gregg attempted once more to persuade Mr De Bear to boldly settle on

Gregg Shorthand, but he would not commit himself. In impatience and disappointment Mr Gregg left the meeting and took a ride on an open-topped bus to clear his mind. Suddenly he got one of his brilliant ideas, and hurried to the Managing Director of the Remington Typewriter office at London. There he proposed to buy all 33 of the De Bear Schools! The man was so surprised that, in Mr Gregg's words 'He nearly fell off his chair—he thought the idea was preposterous'. However, the matter did not end there: when Mr Gregg returned to America he negotiated with the President and Board of the Remington Typewriter Company, and he did buy the chain of English schools.

While in England Mr Gregg travelled much, visiting schools, friends and relatives. His brother Sam had died in 1918, heartbroken after the death of two of his sons in the war; but his brother, Jared, and his family remained in Scotland. It was on the long and monotonous rail journey from London to Glasgow to visit Jared that a humorous incident occurred which gave Mr Gregg so much pleasure to relate in after years.

He found himself in a carriage with only one other occupant, a silent Scots Highlander, who completely ignored him. Being genial and interested in other people, Mr Gregg always made conversation on his travels, but this individual rejected his pleasant observations of the weather and scenery. After hours of silence Mr Gregg could stand it no longer: 'I am an American and my name is Gregg' he said. The Scotsman looked hard at him and said, 'Aye'. After a moment Mr Gregg added: 'Originally my family came from the Highlands of Scotland, when our name was McGreggor'. The Highlander replied only 'Aye'. Trying once again, Mr Gregg said: 'I publish books'. The man then stirred himself, and declared: 'Aye. The McGreggors were always robbers'.

* * *

At the National Shorthand Reporters Association contest, when Billy Rose appeared to challenge the Pitman supremacy there was excitement, for most of the reporters had heard something about his exceptional ability. On the morning of the contest Billy Rose was ill—a form of blood poisoning—and really was in no condition to compete for a world title. But, by a supreme effort of will, he went into the contest-room and successfully took the high-speed dictation; but his strength was exhausted, and as soon as he finished writing, he collapsed. It was hoped that he would recover sufficiently during the day to transcribe his notes which had been removed by an official and sealed. But despite medical attention he did not recover in time to be included in the contest. To the very great surprise of all, Albert Schneider[17] was declared the winner of the Championship—the first Gregg Shorthand writer to achieve that distinction.

Mr Gregg received the news as he travelled home to America on the liner 'Cedric', and he rejoiced very much to know that his system had achieved the supreme accolade of the reporting profession.

CHAPTER NOTES

1. Born 1863.
2. Including: *English Progressive Studies, and Course in Business English,* 1905/6.
3. His first important text was: *Applied Business English,* (1908).
4. Fred Gurtler did more than any other early reporter to overcome the predjudice against Gregg Shorthand in the courts. His colleagues witnessing his skill in fluent writing and effortless reading-back, were among the first to recognise the advantages to the reporter of an integral vowel system.
5. In addition to *Rational Typewriting,* SoRelle gained much respect for *Office Training for Stenographers,* (1911) and *Expert Shorthand Speed Course,* (1910).
6. Elbert Hubbard (1859-1915), drowned when the liner 'Lusitania' was sunk by a German submarine during the first World War. His *Little Journey to the Home of Gregg Shorthand,* 1915, was his last work.
7. Died 1927.
8. It should be remembered that the purchasing power of money was then at least 15 times what it is at the present time.
9. Mr Louis B. Gingell.
10. A measure of the progress made is that in 1907, 207 schools in the Eastern area offered Gregg Shorthand; in 1915, 784 did so.
11. The positions were calculated upon the combined results of speed and accuracy on dictations at 150 to 210 words per minute.
12. Almost every one described Swem's position as 'the President's Secretary'. In fact, that office was held by Mr Tumulty.
13. Mr Gregg encouraged Paula Werning to train for National Shorthand Reporters Association championship contest. She was, in fact, one of the fastest and most accurate writers of all time, but she was exceedingly nervous and did not win the prize when she competed in 1913. She held an important executive position with the Treasury Department at Washington until she was struck down by a fatal illness in 1920.
14. J. G. Cross, John Robert Gregg, Ben Pitman, and W. W. Osgoodby.
15. William Smart, who had received a gold watch from Sir Isaac Pitman in commemoration of his passing a 220 w.p.m. shorthand test, remained in the United States to operate a court reporting office which undertook the record of some of the most difficult patent litigation. He employed a number of the most skilled shorthand writers in America (including several of Mr Gregg's champions,) as well as the fastest typists to transcribe their dictation. Shortly before his death, Mr Smart wrote to JRG: 'You were kindness personified to my sister Ada, also to Mary Carrington [a champion typist] and myself, over many years'.
16. His daughter learned the system so quickly and easily that her father was astonished. Yet Mr De Bear was unable to rid himself of the prejudice of a lifetime, and hesitated to adopt Gregg Shorthand in his schools. His daughter emigrated to America, and worked as a secretary in the Gregg Publishing Company until her marriage.
17. Later, Official Reporter, House of Congress, Washington.

Chapter Seven Triumphs and Tragedy

At the end of the first World War President Wilson again called upon Charles Swem to act as his shorthand writer and personal assistant when he went with the American delegation to the Peace Conference in Europe. Charles Swem was with him at Versailles, and served him until the end of his term of office in 1920. The eight years they had worked together had been mutually beneficial in the highest degree, for the President had the advantage of the services of a perfectionist, and Charles Swem was given undreamed-of opportunities for travel and the experience of the executive life at its highest level. Their relationship was one of mutual respect furthered by the fact that they had several common interests. Both of them delighted in mystery novels, and the President, who could not afford much time for leisure reading, was happy to accept the recommendations of his assistant who read deeply in the new publications of that sort. Latterly, the President encouraged Swem to pursue the two ambitions which he had forgone while in the presidential service: the winning of the World's Championship Shorthand Contest, and a venture into the literary world.

It was with both ambitions in mind that Charles Swem went to Mr Gregg and reminded him of his promise that he would give him the chance to train for the National Shorthand Reporters Association championship contest. Mr Gregg had not forgotten, and by the new commercial year in the autumn of 1921, Swem was engaged as editor of *The Gregg Writer,* and the new journal for teachers, *The American Shorthand Teacher.* As soon as he had settled into these duties, facilities were organised to allow him to practise the legal matter which he had not used since 1912, and the necessary shorthand partner for competition and encouragement was procured.

As the activities of the Gregg Publishing Company expanded, Mr Gregg introduced new staff whose skills seemed appropriate to the challenging opportunities. Clyde Blanchard, who had gained wide renown by his public teaching at the Panama Pacific Exposition of 1915, joined the company for editorial and executive duties. There were also various new travelling representatives whose function was to maintain that close communication with the teachers which was such a marked characteristic of the organisation. Wallace W. Renshaw was one of those who began 'in the field' and gained the experience of the teachers' problems which guided his sympathetic interest throughout his later years at the headquarters. It was within the first few weeks of his long service with the company tht Mr Renshaw made a contact which was highly important to Mr Gregg and the future history of Gregg Shorthand.

In the ardour of his initial enthusiasm, Renshaw called upon the most bigoted Pitmanic shorthand teachers in the most conservative New England locations. One of these, at Greenfield, Mass., was a Miss Cora Ward, impregnable in her conviction that no system could match the Pitmanic adaptation which she taught. She was therefore quite incredulous when Renshaw declared that he could demonstrate the superiority of Gregg Shorthand by his correspondence course alone: let her choose any of her students to work through his correspondence course, and within twelve months that student would out-perform the students who had had the benefit of two years of her personal tuition: As if to dismiss the absurdity of the matter, she turned to a thirteen-year-old boy, Louis A. Leslie, who chanced to be in the room at that moment, while servicing a duplicating machine, and inquired: 'Would you like to learn shorthand'? He did. Fate had brought Renshaw and Gregg Shorthand to a brilliant boy with a gift for shorthand.

After only a few of the specified 12 months were past, Louis A. Leslie had worked through the Gregg Shorthand correspondence course, and naively sought Miss Ward's advice: 'What do I do next'? She replied: 'You learn to write at speed'. And to demonstrate this difficulty, she asked him to attempt to take her dictation of a passage at 40 words a minute, such as she was accustomed to offer her students after a year of her teaching. Although he had never had any shorthand dictation in his life, he took it, and he read it back—very much to her surprise. She then dictated a passage at 50 words per minute, and he read that back also. Truly amazed, Miss Ward finally dictated a passage at 60 w.p.m., and again he read it back with ease. She was utterly dumbfounded. 'It is amazing' was her comment. Immediately afterwards she wrote to Mr Renshaw to say that she was convinced of the merit of Gregg Shorthand and wished to introduce the system at the beginning of the September term.

Three years later Louis A. Leslie attended the Gregg Normal Summer Session at Chicago in preparation for his Teacher's qualification. He was one of those writing in the great lecture room when Mr Gregg came to see their work, just prior to giving his annual inspirational address.[1] He stopped beside the desk, picked up his notebook and scrutinised the pages most carefully, then briefly observed 'That's pretty good shorthand', and moved on. Mr Gregg had once more marked out a person for future employment. Some months later, while teaching in his first position, Louis A. Leslie received a telegram offering him a place with the Gregg Publishing Company—to conduct the Correspondence Course tuition. Louis A. Leslie accepted the position and at seventeen years of age took over the responsibility for the educational programme by which he had first been introduced to Gregg Shorthand.

At New York Mr Gregg, always solicitous for the welfare of the young people in his employment, was particularly concerned for this youth whose father, many years before, had been struck down by yellow fever at the Suez Canal. Mr Gregg was delighted to discover that his new assistant was, like himself, one of those very rare persons who loved shorthand for its own sake, and studied shorthand systems as an intellectual and historical interest. Mr Gregg loved to talk at length upon shorthand; upon the historical relationship of different systems and their technical merits and failings. When the day's work was done, there was scarcely anything he liked more than to recount his early missionary experience and to tell of discussions and debates with the

PAULA E. WERNING

LOUIS A. LESLIE AGED 20

MARTIN J. DUPRAW AGED 16

ALBERT SCHNEIDER AGED 21

enthusiasts for other systems. Unlike the other members of staff, who were bored by such matters, Louis A. Leslie was keenly interested, and had a retentive memory for these reminiscences.

* * *

From the earliest days of Gregg Shorthand, students and teachers would write to Mr Gregg asking for his comments and criticism on pages of their notes. When such correspondence increased beyond his ability to cope with it personally, a separate division of the office was established to help these enquirers, and it in turn grew into the 'Art and Credentials Department'. Individual students, and whole classes studying the system under teachers of private and public schools were encouraged to aim towards a very high standard of theoretical knowledge, penmanship, and practical skills which were acknowledged by the award of a graduated range of certificates, school club prizes and decorative badges. For many years the Art and Credentials Department was conducted by Florence E. Ulrich, who had a particular gift for patient examination and unerring detection of excellence among the enormous number of applicants for the Gregg Awards.[2]

One of the most popular awards was the annual 'Order of the Gregg Artists' which had commenced in 1912. Each year hundreds of thousands of individual students and 'school clubs', hoping to win the coveted certificate, submitted examples of their shorthand transcription of a page of English text which was examined for accuracy of principles and beauty of execution. Particularly skilful groups of students and their teachers were acknowledged by the award of semi-precious OGA pins, and engrossed Honour Rolls, and various useful prizes.

There was also a programme of awards for those who attained a high standard of accuracy in writing and transcribing shorthand from dictation. Certificates were awarded on tests given by teachers in the schoolrooms up to 100 w.p.m., and bronze and silver medals could be won by those who satisfied the examiners' committees at 125 and 150 w.p.m. Tests were conducted at the offices of the Gregg Publishing Company for the 'Expert' awards of gold and diamond medals for the relatively few who achieved the highest standards of performance at 175 and 200 w.p.m.

The programme of examining the candidates for the higher speed awards was conducted by Archibald A. Bowle for many years. He was the son of Mr Gregg's old friend and early pupil, Robert Bowle. When Mr Gregg had learned that Robert Bowle had suffered a terrible road accident and was unable to fulfil his expectations for his son, he came to his assistance and virtually adopted Archibald, bringing him to America in 1911 to stay initially at his household, and providing a place for him in the company.

Throughout his life Mr Gregg retained a deep sense of gratitude to those who had assisted him in the days of his early trials, and he was ever ready to befriend them. An example of his attitude is seen in his treatment of E. N. Miner, who had fared badly since the sale of the *Typewriter and Phonographic*

World. Mr Gregg knew that he was too proud to accept a financial gift or a loan so he inquired if there was any book which Mr Miner wished to write. He got the positive reply that he had it in mind for many years to write a specialised dictionary for secretarial workers. They met and Mr Gregg commissioned him to write the book,[3] and gave him a very large advance on the royalties.[4] With the money Mr Miner established a small commercial school in Oklahoma City where he taught Gregg Shorthand until his death in 1923.

Mr Gregg's behaviour towards his staff was certainly paternalistic. He very rarely fired any one, so that his employees had a comforting sense of security. Yet his early experiences had made him cautious of undue expense, and he did not believe in 'spoiling' young people by paying high salaries too early—he felt that they had first to prove their competence and their earning-power. Some of those who worked for him, or who wished to work for him, considered his offered rewards insufficient. Perhaps he did entertain the suspicion of 'young men in a hurry' held by most persons of middle age and after, but it is certain that he had an extreme dislike of being pressurised by those who had a firm estimate of their own worth, and there were some occasions when his resistance, on principle, lost him the services of persons who later became well-known in the world of education.

He was, however, generous to a fault in the matter of financial assistance to those who worked for him, giving numerous mortgage loans to those who wished to buy their homes. He was also deeply concerned in matters of health, shouldering heavy responsibilities at a time when health insurance was not as widespread as in modern times. Bearing in mind the terrible memory of his sister's death, he several times paid for the long-term stays at sanatoria for young women from his office.

* * *

The headquarters staff coped with a correspondence which was world-wide, for *The Gregg Writer* and *The American Shorthand Teacher* were distributed throughout the English-speaking countries, and the Spanish magazine, *El Taquigrafo Gregg* had a large circulation in the Central and South American countries.

One of the company's Spanish correspondents in 1917 was later to become very well-known. The writer in Cuba inquired about the free correspondence course, and his letter was brought to Louis A. Leslie who found that Fulgencio Batista was not a teacher wishing to teach the system, therefore did not qualify for the free course. He wrote back recommending one of the shorthand classes which were flourishing on the island since the years when Mr Gregg first introduced the study in 1906. Soon there came a further letter, to the effect that Fulgencio Batista was a poverty-stricken youth of 16 who could not possibly afford the commercial school fees, and there was a fervent plea to be considered as a 'special case'. Louis A. Leslie, remembering that he had been made a 'special case', took the request to Mr Gregg, who authorised his cost-free tuition.[5] Few young persons ever made better use of the opportunity. Fulgencio Batista learned the system so thoroughly that he was able to train himself as a court reporter, and joined the army in that capacity. He was later to aver that he owed a great debt to Mr Gregg and his shorthand system, for it contributed substantially to his rise to become the leader of his people in the revolution of 1933.

* * *

After an interval of ten years Charles Swem competed for the NSRA professional championship cup in 1922. He won the second prize in the contest—a very fine achievement for a person who had never done any court reporting in his life. Two other Gregg Shorthand writers distinguished themselves in the tests: Louis A. Leslie, who won the Amateur Championship, and Martin Dupraw, just turned 16, who qualified in the 200 w.p.m. test—an unheard-of achievement for a boy of that age.

The next year Charles Swem competed again, and he won the Championship from a field of 40 entrants. Mr Gregg was exceedingly pleased, and encouraged him to defend his title in the 1924 contest—which he won a second time. That year the Gregg writers rejoiced in another professional honour: Fred Gurtler was elected President of the National Shorthand Reporters Association.

Charles Swem now set his heart upon the ultimate crown of glory at the NSRA. It had been agreed that if any one could ever win the Championship three times in succession, that person would retire the cup.

The tension and excitement was extreme at Omaha on the 17th August, 1925, when Swem battled with the finest shorthand writers of the English-speaking world. The Championship was won by Martin Dupraw, at the age of 19. His transcriptions surpassed all previous records of accuracy by having but a single error in each of the three nerve-shattering high-speed dictations.[6] Charles Swem took the second place in the championships with an accuracy which was slightly lower.[7] In the succeeding years 1926 and 1927, Martin Dupraw won the Championship again, and according to the rules of the contest, he retired the NSRA Championship cup. It was also the end of an era, for the NSRA abandoned the championship contests. When they were revived in 1952, all the contestants were shorthand machine writers. Martin Dupraw was the last NSRA pen-writing champion.

* * *

The first World War had undermined the plans made for the large-scale development of Gregg Shorthand teaching in Britain, but Mr Gregg was determined to implement those intentions, and he returned to the project in 1921. He and Mrs Gregg sailed to England in the early summer, and within a few weeks there was a reorganised English office for the Gregg Publishing Company in London, under the management of Archibald A. Bowle. The campaign had necessarily to be concentrated upon the activities of private schools, for unlike the conditions in America, very few of the public schools

MAIDA WASSON GREGG   JOHN ROBERT GREGG 1921

offered any instruction in commercial subjects. By his purchase in 1922 of the 33 De Bear Schools, Mr Gregg secured at a single stroke the means of launching his system in Britain with a magnitude of activity which otherwise would have taken many years to achieve. As on previous occasions when a chain of schools converted to Gregg Shorthand, a training session was held for the teachers. Mr Gregg led a team of his American instructors at the intensive training held after the conference organised for Mr Bernard De Bear,[8] his school principals, and 200 teachers at Liverpool in July, 1922. Notwithstanding the short period of preparation, in the immediately following terms, the teachers achieved a level of student successes in shorthand in public examinations which exceeded anything in the schools' history.

The affairs of the re-named 'Gregg Schools' and the English publishing company absorbed a large proportion of Mr Gregg's time and energy during the middle 1920s; yet, while in Britain he found time to lend assistance to the Willis-Byrom Club through his contacts with a number of shorthand historians. Since the death of the founder, the scholarly shorthand reporter, Charles Currier Beale, the club had languished, and the members had ceased to maintain their programme of writing. Now Mr Gregg undertook the revival of the club by arranging meetings, and writing for the *Bulletin,* and by urging the completion of various partly-written manuscripts. By his action a valuable monograph[9] was added to the body of literature on shorthand history, as well as several minor works.

Very few men of middle age would have wished— or been able—to maintain the pace and pressure of activity which Mr Gregg continued throughout the 1920s. In Both America and Britain he travelled extensively between his various school and business locations, keeping in touch with his principals and managers and guiding developments in many areas of publishing. His system was adapted to a large number of languages throughout the world during these years: French and German editions of the shorthand textbooks were published in 1924; Polish and Maltese appeared in 1926; and, in the succeeding years Portuguese and Italian and Irish joined the much earlier texts in Spanish and Esperanto. Wherever there was a demand, the publishing company provided the *Manuals*[10] and the auxiliary texts to encourage the local interest. In 1925 Mr Gregg purchased a group of Canadian commercial schools and built upon their potential. Two years later, he opened a Toronto office to consolidate the gains made in that territory.

He continued in such strenuous exertions partly because he liked the excitement of new challenges, and partly because he had never lost the zeal of a missionary to bring the benefits of his beautiful and simple system to as many young people as he could. His own enthusiasm was infectious, so that he was in constant demand as a speaker among both teachers and students in the schools, colleges, and educational conventions. At those places he was asked so often to account for his success in business and educational projects, that he found the subject something of an embarrassment, and latterly was in the habit of summarising his 'success formula' under the headings of five words: Analyse, Organise, Deputise, Standardise, Energise. Nothwithstanding what was implied by this descriptive programme, there was a great deal of personal supervision and personal decision-making required, and much time-consuming study of the reports and communications received from his wide-spread employees. Perhaps the most exhausting of all his problems were those generated in England.

Several of the Gregg Schools were over-staffed, uneconomical, and badly housed; others were run by principals who had probably obtained their positions without adequate qualification during the manpower shortage of the first World War. Most other businessmen would have ruthlessly dismissed the inefficient employees, but Mr Gregg took a more humane approach and tried to improve their performance by example and persuasion. Mr De Bear found it difficult to cooperate with his American co-workers, and when he died in 1924, his successor, as Head of the Gregg Schools, clashed frequently with the manager of the Gregg Publishing Company at London. The manager was then C. I. Brown,[11] whose brash, extrovert behaviour and abrasive manner greatly offended the restrained conventionality of the English teachers. Inevitably Mr Gregg was called upon again and again to make peace between his contending employees, when his time and energy would have been better spent in planning and adminstration. There was also another worrying circumstance: the fees traditionally charged by English commercial schools were very low, and they could not be increased without losing competitiveness with the other private commercial schools. There was little prospect of recovering the purchase price of the 30 schools and for many years Mr Gregg had to accept the fact that his crusade for Gregg Shorthand in Britain was to continue a costly undertaking.

It is fortunate that Mr Gregg cultivated the habit of dismissing business thoughts from his mind when he took recreation. He spent pleasant evenings at his clubs—particularly the National Arts Club in New York—where he was rated very highly as a conversationalist and a proficient adversary in games of pool. His attitude to these evenings was clearly stated in a letter to Raymond Kelley: 'When I go to a club I want to forget all about business and enjoy myself in a social way. I suppose that none of my club friends have the slightest idea of what my business is except that I am a publisher'.

Whenever possible Mr and Mrs Gregg combined their annual travel to Britain with a leisurely pleasure cruise. One which was especially memorable was in June 1925, when they sailed to the Mediterranean on the Red Star line, calling at Funchal on the island of Madeira, Algiers, and Naples, before continuing to London. It was on this cruise that they met Mrs Kate Kinley, the wife of the President of the University of Illinois, and their daughter, Janet. Mr and Mrs Gregg were to continue in friendly correspondence with them.

That year, 1925, brought Mr Gregg two links with his English pioneering days. The Gregg Shorthand convention was held at Stratford-on-Avon, where Mr S. G. Field, as guest of honour, was able to see the fulfilment of his old dream of a convention with hundreds of Gregg Shorthand enthusiasts in his home town, and among them were several of his one-time pupils who had achieved distinction in life through the start which Gregg Shorthand had given them. Also at Stratford-on-Avon, Mr Gregg received a buoyant communication from Fred Spragg, who was 'doing well in the textile business'.

Mr Gregg had to travel to America before he could arrange the meeting which Spragg had requested, but he wrote to congratulate him on his altered circumstances. But no sooner had Mr Gregg reached New York than he received another letter from Spragg which reverted to the old pattern: he was penniless in London, and without a job, and begged Mr Gregg to send him £7 immediately, and to give him temporary employment. Mr Gregg replied 'I received your letter with feelings of depression and regret', but he cabled Mr Brown at his London office to advance the £7 to Spragg, and he arranged for him to work for a time in the publishing company's store.

Spragg did not exert himself, and soon the blunt Mr Brown persuaded him that it would be best for every one if he went elsewhere: After a year Spragg was still at the Gregg Publishing Company; however, he wrote to Mr Gregg that he planned to set up a business in Portugal, and would leave if Mr Gregg could make him a small loan. By January, 1927, the impecunious Spragg was trying to persuade his one-time friend, at a distance of three thousand miles, to purchase his 'stuffed Humming Birds' to raise a little more cash before sailing to Portugal.

Great preparations were made for the 1928 Gregg Shorthand convention in England, which was to celebrate the 40th anniversary of John Robert Gregg's *Light-Line Phonography* in the city of Liverpool where it was published exactly 40 years before. Maida Gregg insisted on travelling to England although she had been far from well during much of the previous year. At Liverpool she was taken ill with a severe cold which led to pleurisy, and was followed by pneumonia. She was too ill to attend the anniversary dinner. What should have been such a joyful occasion for Mr Gregg was clouded by the death of his brother Jared a few days before, and by his anxiety about Maida's health.

At the dinner two very fine gifts were made to Mr Gregg. The first was a beautiful leather-bound book containing testimonials from friends, colleagues, and members of the Gregg Association of Britain; the second was from the staff and students of the Gregg schools, a sumptuous gold and enamelled casket decorated with illustrations of the history of shorthand from Tironian Notes of c. 50BC to the modern outlines represented by Gregg Shorthand. In his speech of acceptance and thanks, Mr Gregg took the opportunity of reminiscing about his youthful struggles in Liverpool, and of the first years of the existence of Gregg Shorthand.[12]

* * *

Tragically, Maida Gregg died at London on the 28th June, 1928.

Terribly shocked by his bereavement, Mr Gregg sailed to New York with Maida's body, a return in sorrow which swept away all memory of the triumphal outward journey two months before.

Maida Gregg's funeral service was held in New York City, July 12, in the Church of the Transfiguration, East Twenty-Ninth Street, and attended by several hundred friends including many prominent creative people from the world of Literature, Art, and Drama, and many from Educational circles, as well as members of The National Arts Club and The Twelfth Night Club. The Episcopalian service, in compliance with Maida Gregg's wish, was similar to that for O. Henry, who had been buried from the same church in 1910, and the choir sang, as then, 'Crossing the Bar', 'Abide With Me', and 'Peace, Perfect Peace'.

The appalling loss that he had suffered was in part expressed by Mr Gregg when he spoke of his debt to Maida at the 40th Birthday celebrations at Liverpool:

> I gladly and gratefully acknowledge that I owe much of whatever success I have had to her. She has been beside me—not behind me—for the last 29 years. From the moment we married success seemed to come my way. I attribute that very largely to her wise counsel, her sympathy in good times and bad times, and her admonitions'.

CHAPTER NOTES

1. Of these addresses given over so many years, this seems to be the only one which has survived. It was reported by Louis A. Leslie, and was subsequently published with appropriate illustrations as: *Some Young People Who Made Good—And Why.*

109

2. The awards programme proved to be a valuable stimulus to shorthand study, and a considerable proportion of students took part. Some idea of the scale of operations can be gathered from the fact that in the early 1920s there were nearly 750,000 new Gregg learners per year, and those figures increased each session.

3. *Vocabulary Studies for Stenographers,* 1922. A well-written book, but, unfortunately, not popular. It fell between the interests of the commercial student and the working secretary.

4. Information from Dr Louis A. Leslie, who was present at this meeting.

5. The course, and all the correspondence, was sent out under the name of John Robert Gregg.

6. In the three dictations of 200, 240, and 280 w.p.m., Martin Dupraw's accuracy was 99.91%

7. 99.69%

8. Mr De Bear was won over to the system at a demonstration by Raymond Kelley, in 1919. He then wrote on the blackboard, with ease, the most difficult dictation at 200 w.p.m., and afterwards read back fluently to his audience of teachers. Mr De Bear, remembering his own agonising attempts to capture such a speed, had commented: 'I have had a lifetime of experience with shorthand, ... I am bound to say I have never seen a speed performance of any kind equal that of Mr Kelley in the writing of 200 w.p.m. on a blackboard, with new straight matter from a strange reader, and right up to the date of the demonstration I should have scouted even the possibility of such a performance'. (*Gregg Writer,* July 1919, p. 507).

9. *John Willis,* by Alexander Tremaine Wright, published by the Willis Byrom Club, 1926.

10. The Gregg Shorthand textbook was invariably known as *The Manual* by the students and teachers.

11. The nephew of G. W. Brown, the highly successful school proprietor, whose adoption of Gregg Shorthand had assisted Mr Gregg's fortune in earlier years.

12. Mr Gregg never wrote a history of Gregg Shorthand; however it became customary with him to give some account of the history of his shorthand at conventions in America and Britain. He spoke without notes and introduced only such portions of the story as he felt appropriate to the particular gathering. The majority of those talks did not appear in the official proceedings. Fortunately, after 1917, Dr Louis A. Leslie was present at the most important conventions, and he took a shorthand record of these reminiscences. He amalgamated these talks into a historical account, *Gregg Shorthand —Its Early History,* which was revised and approved by Mr Gregg. It is published in *The Story of Gregg Shorthand,* (published by McGraw-Hill Book Company, 1964) which is a collection of some of the writing of John Robert Gregg, edited by Dr Louis A. Leslie.

Chapter Eight Domesticity and Deserved Rewards

In an effort to divert his thoughts from the depressing loneliness of his condition, Mr Gregg entered upon a great deal of intensive activity. He might have preoccupied himself with the many responsibilities of the magazine and textbook production, but he could not settle to such work, and even developed a distaste for the few really essential business visits to the Chicago and New York offices. He involved himself much in the National Art Club business, and that temporarily took precedence over his publishing and educational commitments. It was a time when there were few friends or relatives at hand to share sorrow, for not only had he now lost his brothers, but Fate had recently taken from him several of his closest friends and acquaintances; among them were A. N. Palmer, who had died in 1926, and Fred Gurtler, who fell a victim to sudden illness in December, 1928, at the age of 41.

For two years Mr Gregg travelled frequently and extensively, much of it in connection with voluntary service which he gave to a variety of professional associations in America and Europe. In August, 1928, he attended the convention of the National Shorthand Reporters Association at Minneapolis, where he took part, with Helen Evans, in the Gregg Clinic, the discussion and exchange of ideas concerning reporting vocabulary and methods. Mr Gregg, who was one of the seven surviving Charter Members of the NSRA, delivered an important talk on 'Mental and Manual Factors which affect Shorthand Speed'. Afterwards he continued to the University of Illinois, in response to a long-standing invitation from President and Mrs Kinley to visit them, and to renew his acquaintance with their daughter, Janet. Other journeys took him late in the summer to Hannibal, Missouri, to settle Maida's affairs, and afterwards to California on a tour of educational institutes.

In 1929 Mr Gregg was honoured by Bryant College, Providence, Rhode Island, where he received the degree of Master of Commercial Science. He was also honoured by the Department of State, being designated 'American Delegate' to the International Congress for Commercial Education at Amsterdam. After his work in Holland, Mr Gregg continued to London, where he advised on the complex business affairs of the Gregg Publishing Company in England, now operating with H. L. Carrad, as Managing Director, and Mr Addington Symons, as General Editor. Like the chain of Gregg Schools in Britain, the publishing company continued to require a major financial subsidy from the profits of the American organisation. Notwithstanding his disinclination to be drawn into the problems of the business, Mr Gregg was obliged to concentrate his energy to some extent upon ways of reducing the very considerable losses being made each year—a financial condition which in no way reflected the continuing successes of the Gregg Shorthand students in the independently administered national commercial examinations.

Amidst many worries and irritations there was one particular circumstance which uplifted his spirit: he found that there was a widening band of enthusiasts among the intellectuals of the country, and their letters to him raised fresh hope that his dream of Gregg Shorthand replacing ordinary longhand among professional people might yet be realised. One of his most interesting correspondents was a young journalist who worked as an educational officer in the Salvation Army, Captain Thomas Winter. He had recently been converted to Gregg Shorthand and was so enthusiastic about the benefits which the system had brought to him that he was anxious to introduce it officially into the Salvation Army training college. He put forward various recommendations to Mr Gregg, who wrote to Winter to tell of Gregg Shorthand's earlier associations with the Salvation Army through Spragg, his first pupil, and George Watson, and he expressed his pleasure at learning that another Salvationist was proposing to further the interests of the system, and he sent him an invitation to attend the next meeting of the Metropolitan Gregg Shorthand Association. Winter, in turn, wrote[1] that he was a regular contributor to the Salvation Army periodical, *The War Cry,* and wished to write an appreciation of Gregg Shorthand in one of his articles, and requested a little of Mr. Gregg's shorthand which he could reproduce as an example. But he could not attend the meeting:

I am very sorry to say I shall not be able to be present as I shall be in the country on 21st September. Most of my life is spent in trains and I am almost too busy to make time even for the more ordinary pleasures (so-called); but I would not exchange my 24-hour-a-day job for any of the occupations of which I hear. I am afraid I am incurably in love with Work; however, you shall have every scrap of proselytizing zeal I possess. Up in Sunderland the other day I bought a 'Victory'[2] Manual and presented it to an officer who was writhing under the Pitman visitation: at Yalding last week I converted another, and two other friends of mine now have Manuals plus many hours of enjoyment as a result of my own encouraging experience. May the shade of Isaac[3] forgive me:

When I read in the monthly the report of the Annual Dinner and the remarks about your sad loss, in which I pray God may sustain you, I said to my wife: 'This man is loved': To my mind there will never be a higher tribute which will be paid you.

Your system inspires gratitude, and, if my experience is anything by which to go, contact with you is productive of affection. You must forgive a young man speaking in this fashion. I wish to God I could be as sure of laying down my head in complete satisfaction at a good work well done as you may justly do every night of your life. It is not possible, of course, to say any comforting word at this time; I am happily married myself and it is terrible to imagine life alone. But I shall pray for you in my own unorthodox manner.

After an extended visit to Cuba, Mr Gregg returned to receive a letter from Boston University advising him that they wished to confer upon him the honorary degree of Doctor of Commercial Science (Sc.D) and they invited him to receive it on the 16th June, 1930. He attended on that date, and at the degree ceremony he met Janet Kinley once again. She was present as the guest of her older sister who was graduating that day with a higher degree. There was much to talk about, and that evening Janet Kinley and Mr Gregg dined together on this happy occasion.

Mr Gregg spent the remainder of the summer in Britain. He returned to New York in the Autumn to supervise the move of headquarters staff into the luxurious new suite of offices at 270 Madison Avenue. The extensive accommodation, wood-panelled in Jacobean style, was formerly used by a leading silk merchant to display his rich materials, and it seemed particularly appropriate that the home of the very elegant Gregg Shorthand should be located in such surroundings. Mr Gregg's spacious office was above the corner of Madison Avenue and 39th Street, illuminated by large leaded-glass casement windows furnished with thick apple-green hangings, and the walls were decorated with oil paintings brought from his own collection. The move to this beautiful office marked the return of Mr Gregg's zest for work, and his renewed interest in the preparation of the numerous textbooks on commercial subjects and reporting practice which made such a valuable contribution to education in the 1930s.

On the morning of October 22nd, Mr SoRelle and Mr Hagar were greatly surprised when Mr Gregg took leave of them at the office and told them that he was to be married two days later at Gallup, New Mexico, to Janet Kinley. The wedding was to be quiet, and he asked them to discourage publicity. The national press, however, could not be dissuaded from printing photographs and columns after the event.

Very soon letters and cables of congratulation arrived in great numbers from Mr Gregg's personal friends and acquaintances, as well as well-wishers throughout the world. To many of these Mr Gregg replied personally. To Raymond Kelley he wrote on December 4, 1930:

It has been a lonesome life the past two years, and at times very depressing. That is why I have been travelling so much. Now I am very happy in having a home life again.

* * *

By the later 1920s there was an urgent need for a revised textbook: the younger teachers did not like the emphasis on abbreviated outlines which had been introduced into the 1916 *Manual*. The majority of the teachers, at the time it was prepared, were converts from Pitmanic systems which employed extremely abbreviated outlines as an essential feature, and they could not rid themselves of the belief that these were necessary for shorthand speed. By the 1920s a wealth of experience had disproved such convictions, and it was clear that the ordinary secretarial worker did not require to memorise so many special shorthand word beginnings and endings. There was also a general demand for a textbook with practice matter that was more in keeping with the current interests of the young people learning shorthand.

Mr Gregg began the revision in 1927 and engaged the assistance of Rupert SoRelle, who had done sterling work on so many of the Gregg Publishing Company educational texts, including the 1916 *Manual*. The totally unexpected circumstances of Mr Gregg's life during the preparation of the revision resulted in a greater and greater delegation of responsibility to SoRelle, and that was to have the most serious consequences.

Mr Gregg had associated Mr SoRelle in the revision of the *Manual* because he wished the work to be carried out quickly: it was intended that it would be published on the 40th anniversary of the system, and was to be called *The Anniversary Edition*—but even more importantly, he was motivated by an act of kindness: he wanted to give Mr SoRelle an activity which would divert his mind from a terrible series of tragedies which had cast him into a state of despondency.

Mr and Mrs SoRelle had three sons. The youngest, when 16 years of age, caught a chill at a Boy Scout camp and died of pneumonia; the second died suddenly of another disease; and the third committed suicide when under the influence of deep depression. Mrs SoRelle, whose kindly lovable nature endeared her to every one, died of a long and painful illness in 1926. Although nearly overwhelmed by this succession of misfortunes, Rupert SoRelle attempted to recover something of his former domestic happiness, and he married again. Unfortunately, he married the wrong person: the second Mrs SoRelle was quite unlike the gentle, affectionate lady who was his first partner, and the the marriage was very unsuccessful. These troubles were too much for Mr SoRelle to bear, and his physical condition and his great intellectual powers were undermined.

Mr Gregg, however, did not realise how deeply SoRelle was affected when he delegated to him such matters as the arrangement of the principles, the shorthand vocabulary, and the continuous material of the *Anniversary Edition Manual;* and, afflicted by grief in 1928, he could not concentrate on the supervision of SoRelle's work. When the textbook appeared in May, 1929, the Gregg Shorthand teachers were exceedingly disappointed by the dullness of the text, and they quickly discovered a multitude of inconsistencies, and inaccuracies in the examples. The other members of the editorial staff hurried through a 'second printing' of the Anniversary Manual and an article in *The Gregg Writer*[4] explained away various 'printer's errors' and unfortunate slips. The textbook never won favour with those who used it, and another revision would certainly have come quickly from Mr Gregg, had it not been for the economic Depression of the 1930s which greatly inhibited the purchase of textbooks by the schools.

The school officials and teachers of Latin-America entertained Mr Gregg at a 'Good-Will Luncheon' in New York city on May 9th, 1931. They wished to honour him in recognition of his outstanding contribution to commercial education, and more that 350 people were in attendance. They brought, and presented to him, the gift of a testimonial signed by thousands of others who could not join them. That testimonial was mounted in a beautiful leather cover having a profile of Mr Gregg stamped in gold. With it was an illuminated 'Scroll of Honour' bearing the signatures of a thousand teachers in Central and South America, Mexico, and the West Indies. Mr Gregg was deeply moved by their expression of appreciation, and he was delighted by the adoption of his birthday, June 17, as a holiday and feast day in Latin-American schools: 'Dia de Gregg'.

In October 1932 Mr and Mrs Gregg moved to their new home in the beautiful apartment at One Lexington Avenue, overlooking Gramercy Park, on the other side of which is situated The National Arts Club. On November 10th their daughter, Kate Kinley, was born.

During the next year or two Mr Gregg was much occupied with the affairs of The National Arts Club, and the 'Players' next door, and the Gramercy Park Association. They would have been tranquil years but for the effects of the Depression. He did a great deal to alleviate the difficulties of both institutions and acquaintances in the world of Art and the Theatre. He gave very substantial financial assistance to The National Arts Club; acted as an 'Angel' to Mr and Mrs Coburn in their production of *The Plutocrat;* commissioned an oil portrait of himself from an impecunious painter, Sidney Dickinson; and similarly, had a relief plaque of Janet and her baby made by the sculptor, Poppeo Coppini.

The Depression brought many formerly prosperous persons into need, and they included several of Maida's close friends, and various former members of Mr Gregg's staff, and one very prominent authority in the Pitmanic shorthand world. When they approached him for assistance, he never failed to help them, frequently lending considerable sums of money without any real prospect of it being returned. The Gregg Publishing Company and the Gregg School were both seriously hit by the Depression, but they were able to continue without a single person being fired from the staff: When Raymond Kelley inquired how he was coping with the difficult times,[5] Mr Gregg replied: 'I didn't escape the effects of the crash. If I hadn't put something substantial aside for a "Rainy Day" it would have been a sad story indeed'.

During the early 1930s Mr Gregg put into effect a plan which he had long held in reserve: he began the writing of a comprehensive history of shorthand. He had always found the study of history interesting, and the history of shorthand was to him its most fascinating branch. Since his youth he had collected systems of shorthand from all nationalities, so that he had by then one of the finest collections in the world to provide a source of materials for his writing.

Early in the first World War, Mr Gregg had learned that Carl Mares was preparing a history of shorthand, and remembering his very satisfactory *History of the Typewriter,* he negotiated to purchase the copyright, believing that it would be suitable for serialising in *The Gregg Writer.* However, when the manuscript arrived—years later—he found that it was a dull succession of descriptions of systems without much organisation or commentary, and he realised that he would have to do the work himself. The intervening years were exceedingly busy, so that he did not find the necessary leisure until 1933. The first chapter of the history was printed in *The Business Education World* in September, 1933; thereafter other chapters appeared at intervals until 1936.[6]

* * *

The continuing dissatisfaction with *The Anniversary Manual* was to some extent kept in check by the fact that there were offered at the same time, or immediately afterwards, a number of alternative Gregg Shorthand textbooks, which although synchronised with *The Anniversary Manual,* stressed a particular method of instruction. For a time some of the more progressive teachers experimented with the *Direct Method*[7] (which emphasised the imitation of the teacher's outlines, and encouraged rapid writing from the very beginning), or the *Analytical Method*[8] (which emphasised a close study of the different joinings of characters). But the alternative which attracted the greatest attention was Louis A. Leslie's *Functional Method.*[9] This approach provided the student with a familiarity with Gregg Shorthand outlines by means of reading practice—without any writing whatsoever—until the student had finished the fourth chapter of *The Anniversary Manual.* Unlike the other approaches, no formal theory was taught, for the underlying principle was that the student was never required to write an outline until thoroughly prepared to write it correctly—the correct form having been impressed on the mind by much reading. Although daring in its conception and challenging many of the accepted teaching principles used throughout the country, the method had been proved effective in various experiments[10] and trial classes before it was announced in *The Business Education World* of March 1935.

During the 1930s there was a considerable increase in the proportion of students who wished to take their skills beyond the levels which were expected in ordinary secretarial practice. Those advanced students were initially served only by the articles which appeared monthly in *The Gregg Writer* where Fred Gurtler's Reporting Section had been continued by Charles Swem.[11] In quick succession there appeared a series of textbooks which could guide the student from the 120 words per minute stage to the higher reporting speeds. The most helpful of Charles Swem's articles were gathered together and supplemented by specialist legal and medical vocabularies, and a progressive text, and the work was issued as *The Gregg Reporting Course* in 1936. This extremely influential book was provided with very beautiful shorthand notes, written from dictation by Mr Charles E. Zoubek,[12] a member of staff of the Gregg Publishing Company and a New York Certified Shorthand Reporter. *The Gregg Reporting Course* was designed to be used in conjunction with three advanced dictation books compiled by Louis A. Leslie:[13] *Congressional Dictation, Testimony Dictation,* and *Jury-Charge Dictation.* Together they offered a course of professional training which was unequalled by any other publications in the shorthand world.

* * *

Throughout the later 1930s Mr Gregg continued to supervise the activities of his publishing company, and to make the visits to schools and colleges which in the past had occupied so much of his time. They were, however, less frequent and less extended as his senior executives were able to relieve him of some of these duties. He spent more time with his family, which was augmented on

April 25, 1935, when John Robert Gregg Junior was born. To give the children the advantage of playing in the countryside, and to allow their parents to enjoy peace not to be had in busy New York, Mr Gregg in 1937 purchased a Colonial-style residence surrounded by an estate of unspoilt land at Wilton, Connecticut. Mr Gregg renamed the property 'The Ovals'.[14]

With more leisure at his disposal Mr Gregg applied a considerable portion of his energy to unobtrusive philanthropic work. He instituted scholarships for young people in several fields, including music—which he could never fully enjoy himself on account of his defective hearing—and court reporting at the Gregg School at Chicago; and he supported the Mechanics and Tradesmens School, which catered for the orphans and underprivileged youngsters of New York.[15]

Many honours came to Mr Gregg during these years, but one which he particularly valued was a medal awarded for his accomplishments 'as Author, Publisher, Educator, and Humanist' from the Ulster-Irish Society, in March, 1936, for 'Notable Service to the Nation'.

In July 1937, he attended the International Shorthand Conference at London, England, as the leader of the American delegation. There he received an unexpected commemorative memorial when all those Americans present signed a tribute to him, written in beautiful Gregg Shorthand.[16]

To John Robert Gregg, in commemoration of the 50th anniversary of Gregg Shorthand, we Americans present at this memorable International Shorthand Congress in London, take great pleasure in extending our heartiest congratulations and sincere good wishes to you. To your genius thousands of our shorthand teachers and millions of our shorthand writers owe their thanks and appreciation. Our tremendous shorthand progress, of which we in America are so proud, is altogether the result of your great work.

We take off our hats to you in the real American way and we are proud to be able to claim you as an adopted son of America.

May you and yours enjoy health happiness and prosperity for many years to come. We Americans at this congress are proud to sign this informal but sincere memorial written in London July 24, 1937.

* * *

Mr and Mrs Gregg and the children sailed to England on the *Queen Mary,* and a few days later, on June 4 attended the banquet at London which was to mark the 50th anniversary of the publication of Gregg Shorthand. Over 500 guests were present to demonstrate their loyalty to the system and its inventor. One of the finest tributes to Mr Gregg was made by Sir Walter Citrine,[17] president of the International Federation of Trade Unions, who was an early student of Gregg Shorthand at Liverpool, and who had used the system in his work throughout his highly successful career. The highlight of the evening was the presentation to Mr Gregg of a memento of the Golden Jubilee: a solid gold case, decorated with a relief of Mr Gregg in the centre, and a border of names

LOUIS A. LESLIE   MR. GREGG   CHARLES E. ZOUBEK

and dates of the great shorthand inventors beginning with Marcus Tullius Tiro, and ending with John Robert Gregg. When opened, the case contains a duplicate of the alphabet of Gregg Shorthand copyrighted on March 29, 1888, and an inscription addressed to:

> John Robert Gregg, Doctor of Commercial Science, Inventor, Educationalist, Author, Historian, Patron and Lover of the Arts.

In America a great celebration was under way for their homecoming, and this took place in New York city at the Hotel Commodore on October 8th. Then a succession of speakers who represented teachers, educationalists, reporters, and friends who had benefited from the system, paid their respect to Mr Gregg. A particularly warm tribute was given by Charles Swem, and another equally gratifying, was sent by Fulgencio Batista, then the First Citizen of Cuba, who sent not only a message of gratitude and good-will, but an Amethyst ring engraved with two names: *Batista* and *Gregg*.

* * *

The second World War brought many problems for the Gregg Publishing

118

Company when members of staff were drafted into the armed forces and materials were in short supply. Once again special short-course editions of the textbooks were produced and various war emergency texts were hurried through the press. However, those difficulties were by no means as serious as those which befell the British division of the company. In Britain all the teachers and members of staff under the age of 51 were drafted into the armed forces, and most of the students were evacuated from the larger towns, and several of the schools were destroyed by bombing raids. As though by a malignant Fate, so much of what had been built up with great effort was ruined once more. Both the publishing company and the schools continued to function throughout the war, but at a lower level of activity, and the profitable position which had been reached for the first time in 1939 was converted again into loss. During these war years Mr Gregg took part in a great deal of voluntary work for the welfare of both the Allied forces and the British civilians, services which were acknowledged at the end of the war by King George VI, who awarded him his 'Medal for Service in the Cause of Freedom'.

In August 1942 Mr Gregg visited Springfield, Illinois, to make a recording of his voice and to relate some of his experiences at the request of the American Pioneer Guild. At Springfield he was presented with a commemorative book inscribed: 'John Robert Gregg, distinguished contributor to American life, we have this 8th day of August 1942, dedicated the voice recording of your life, experiences and accomplishments as a lasting memento to the posterity of the Americas'. A few days later, on August 14th Mr Gregg attended the commencement exercises at Rider College, Trenton, New Jersey, where the Vice-President conferred upon him the honorary degree of Doctor of Letters, and in his address recalled that it was Mr Gregg who had reconciled the two men who had been responsible for developing the institution which was then recognising his contribution to Education.

Whenever he was not at his Connecticut home, Mr Gregg continued to work at his office where he answered his very large correspondence—in shorthand, which was subsequently transcribed by his secretary, Margaret Richards. By then his contributions to *The Gregg Writer* were occasional, but his 'Learner's Department' was taken over by Mrs Janet Gregg, who wrote consistently helpful articles during the 1940s.

At his office one morning in January, 1947, Mr Gregg was greatly surprised to find a letter from Fred Spragg. He had not heard anything of him since 1927, and up to that time did not even know if he was still alive. Poor Spragg wrote from a Salvation Army hostel, having been rescued as a derelict from the London streets. He asked Mr Gregg to allow him a pension of $5 a month. Mr Gregg remembered Spragg's natural gifts and the weakness of character which had so undermined his chances of success in life. But the time for admonition and reproach was past, and now Spragg was old, broken, and helpless. He wrote: 'You asked me to arrange to send $5 a month. I am glad to do so on account of old times sentiment.' He also met his request for a copy of the latest Gregg Shorthand *Manual* and added that he enclosed a cheque for £10 ($50) 'As a New Year gift to help with any immediate difficulties you may have.'

On June 17th, 1947, Mr Gregg's 80th birthday, there was a huge mail from well-wishers throughout the world, a great many of the letters coming from young students who were studying the system. But there were also letters from all his surviving old friends, including Louis Pfeiffer, Raymond Kelley, and all the Gregg Shorthand champions. There were also greetings by radio. Among the cables which particularly delighted him was the four-page message from Isaac James Pitman at London, England, and the characteristic Billy Rose communication which ran: 'I understand you'll be 80 years young on June 17. Happy birthday. My congratulations on a long and fine life. Your faith in me some 30 years ago meant OH so much. Affectionate regards, Billy Rose.'

Mr Gregg joined a small group of his friends who celebrated with him at a birthday lunch at the Advertising Club, then he returned to The Ovals to spend the rest of the day with Mrs Gregg and the children. To the newspaper reporters who insisted that he give them his formula for a long and happy life, he replied simply: 'Be interested in everything and everybody'.

On October 22, 1947, Mr Gregg visited the Teachers' College of Connecticut, where he told 200 teachers something of the history of Gregg Shorthand. At the end of this he made the first public announcement of the fact that he was working on a revision of the Gregg *Manual*.[18] This undertaking had been postponed during the war emergency; afterwards, he put a great deal of effort into the preparation of an exposition of the principles which removed some of the features which the students found difficult in the *Anniversary Manual*. He explained that the new *Manual* would contain fewer abbreviations for frequently-used words, and fewer disjoined prefixes and suffixes, and an easier rule for the 'reversed R', and the method of indicating the past tense would be simplified. This announcement was welcomed, and the news spread to educational institutions across the country.

In December 1947 Mr Gregg entered hospital for a serious operation. He made a good recovery from the surgery, and within a short time was writing shorthand replies to his correspondents from his hospital bed. He returned to the Ovals at Wilton, in January 1948, and there continued planning for the new *Manual*.[19] He appeared to be winning the struggle to regain health, but he suffered a heart attack, and passed away on February 23rd, 1948. It was only a few weeks before the 60th Anniversary of Gregg Shorthand.

Mr Gregg's friends and acquaintances were stunned, and greatly saddened, for he had been so vigorous, buoyant and enthusiastic—almost defying the weakness of increasing age. After the first shock there came reflection and gratitude for the experience of having worked with him, or having known him. His life had been exceptionally rich in personal achievement and bequests to others. He had lived to see most of his ambitions realised, and had the satisfaction of knowing that he had secured recognition for his system in America within a few years, essentially by his own efforts, and it had progressed year by year, until latterly Gregg Shorthand was offered in more than 99% of the schools where commercial subjects were taught.

He had provided thousands of shorthand reporters with an invention which was their sole source of livelihood; he had lightened the labour of scores of

MRS FRANCES EFFINGER-RAYMOND   MR GREGG   MRS JANET GREGG

thousands of shorthand teachers, and tens of millions of shorthand students. He was held in affection by almost all who knew him personally, and esteemed and respected by those who knew him only through his writing—and that writing extended beyond the textbooks and magazines, which he had edited for more than 50 years, to include the important contribution to the literature of shorthand history, *The Story of Shorthand.* He was an educator who had the rare ability to teach effectively without making the process of instruction in the least obvious. Like the traditional old family doctor, he was always ready to help with sage advice given with good humour, and was throughout his life the very good friend to innumerable members of the teaching profession.

Undoubtedly it was due to his own genius for organisation and promotional zest that his system and his business achieved such extraordinary success; but it is equally certain that it was his force of personality, benevolence, optimism and enthusiasm which enabled him to retain the services of those outstandingly skilled people who gathered around him, and who worked with such loyalty for him and the cause of Gregg Shorthand.

Among the excellent tributes which were paid to John Robert Gregg, none is more appropriate than that of Leona White in the *National Shorthand Reporter:*[20]

> Through hard work and exceptional mental capacity, he built upon this earth during his lifetime a monument that time can never obliterate or diminish, in whole or in part. . . .
>
> Mortal man does not possess a measuring device adequate to measure the good that he accomplished on this earth. Generations yet unborn will profit from his busy life and accomplishments.

CHAPTER NOTES

1. Thomas Winter to JRG, September, 18, 1929.
2. *Victory Edition,* the special war-time textbook.
3. Sir Isaac Pitman.
4. May, 1930, p.401.
5. Raymond Kelley to JRG, September, 1932.
6. The series was never reprinted in full, but a 128-page selection was issued by the Gregg Publishing Company in 1939.
7. *Direct Method Materials for Gregg Shorthand,* Ann Brewington and Helen I. Soutter, 1933.
8. *Teaching By The Analytical Method,* Minnie De Motte Frick, 1931.

9. *The Teaching of Gregg Shorthand by the Functional Method,* Louis A. Leslie, 1935.

10. The first person to benefit by the method was Charles Rader, who learned Gregg Shorthand by the Functional Method under Louis A. Leslie's instruction, and subsequently became the longest-serving plate writer in the history of Gregg Shorthand. His beautiful, bold, and consistently perfectly-formed outlines appear in Gregg textbooks and magazines for 45 years.

11. In 1925, Charles Swem won the first place in the competitive examinations for the most desirable court reporting positions at New York. Although he left the Gregg Publishing Company to take up a position at the Supreme Court, New York, he continued to contribute his monthly articles to *The Gregg Writer.*

12. In addition to supplying many elegant shorthand illustrations to textbooks and *The Gregg Writer,* Charles Zoubek wrote a number of books for advanced writers: the best-known is the *Expert Shorthand Speed Course.* He is also co-author (with John Robert Gregg and Louis A. Leslie) of the *Gregg Shorthand Manual Simplified,* and subsequent editions of the Manual.

13. Dr Louis A. Leslie is also a New York 'Certified Shorthand Reporter'.

14. This was a play on the name of the curved shape from which most of the Gregg Shorthand characters were taken. In strict accuracy, that shape is an ellipse, but was always loosely described as 'oval'.

15. One of the most inspiring talks which he gave before the young people of this institution, in April 1935, is recorded in their Report for the year. His purpose was to convince them that it is possible to rise above difficult circumstances: he told the story of the achievements of Emil Trefzger, and of the great electrical genius, Steinmetz, and something of his own history.

16. Written by Louis A. Leslie.

17. Later, Lord Citrine.

18. *Beaconson Business Education,* January 22, 1948.

19. *Gregg Shorthand Manual Simplified,* 1949, by John Robert Gregg, Louis A. Leslie, and Charles E. Zoubek.

20. Leona White, (Secretary of the Indiana Shorthand Reporters Association) *National Shorthand Reporter,* April 1948, p.234.

Index